PARSON'S GREEN

'The irregular triangle'

SUE AND LANCE PIERSON

FULHAM AND HAMMERSMITH
HISTORICAL SOCIETY

Books by Sue Pierson

FAIRSEAT

The story of a house and its occupants over the last 400 years

ST MATTHEW'S, FULHAM 1895-1995

PETERBOROUGH SCHOOL 1901-2001

CHARLOTTE SULIVAN 1824-1911: 'The best friend we have'

PETERBOROUGH HOUSE:

'A mansion in every way calculated for a family of distinction'

Published by
The Fulham & Hammersmith Historical Society
https://fhhs.wordpress.com

ISBN 978-0-901643-07-0

Printed by Biddles Books Limited, King's Lynn, Norfolk

Cover Picture:

Parson's Green in 2021 photographed by Sue Pierson

PARSON'S GREEN

IN a Village where I've been
They keep their Parson on a Green.
They tie him to a Juniper Tree
And bring him Currant Bread for tea.
A jollier man I've never seen
Than the one on Parson's Green.

From Eleanor Farjeon's 'Nursery Rhymes of London Town', first volume published 1916.

Illustration by Macdonald Gill.

Acknowledgments

Sue writes: Having written a book about Peterborough House in 2013, I became interested in the other residents of Parson's Green. I started my research in 2015 but could give little time to it. I did not finish writing it up for some years, and then lost heart over how to get it published. I turned to my husband Lance, who has edited other books, and he took over – not only the editing, but he got interested in developing the research himself. He has also done all the hard work of getting this into print. I couldn't have done it without him.

Nor without the encouragement of the Fulham and Hammersmith Historical Society committee. Apart from all the people we acknowledge and quote in the pages that follow, we are also grateful for the help of:

- Kath Shawcross at the Borough Archives
- The patient staff at the London Metropolitan Archives and the Guildhall Library
- Maya Donelan for her interest in the project and identifying helpful sources
- Jenny Whittle and Leila Abu-Sharr for information about St Dionis'
- Vernon Burgess for his interest in the project and alerting us to the story of Heathman's Road
- Kate Wise for information about Lilyville Surgery
- Maureen Grimwood for helping us with the history of Lady Margaret School
- Andrew Harris of the City Pub Co. for information about Aragon House, where he is Manager

- Rev. Gary Piper, former Honorary Chaplain of the Fulham Branch of the Royal British Legion for his advice
- John Hampshire for typing the first draft of the manuscript

All the illustrations in the book are copyright and may not be reproduced without permission. The poem on page3 is reproduced by permission of David Highgam Associates Ltd. The photographs on pages 6, 10, 13, 26, 28, 30 and 37 are in the London Borough of Hammersmith and Fulham Archives. The drawings on pages 16, 40 and 46 are from Keith Whitehouse's personal archive, reproduced with many thanks. The portrait on page 18 is from the Holbein website. The illustration on page 24 is from Grace's Guide to British Industrial History. The photographs on pages 32 and 33 are taken from Brian Owen's "... *a particularly happy place*", by permission of Mrs Elizabeth Owen. The painting on page 39 is reproduced by permission of Tate Images. The portrait on page 41 is reproduced by permission of Christ's Hospital School. The portrait on page 43 is reproduced by permission of the Royal Museums Greenwich. The portraits on pages 45, 49, 55 and 60 are reproduced, courtesy of the National Portrait Gallery. The Rocque map on page 68 is reproduced from *Fulham Old and New volume I* by CJ Fèret and the illustrations on pages10 and 54 from volume 2; the Ordnance Survey maps on pages 69, 70 and 71 are from London sheet 99 of the Godfrey Edition. The illustration on page 48 is from the London Metropolitan Archives.

The north end of Parson's Green with 'The White Horse', c. 1888-91

Londoners in the 21st century appreciate their green spaces as much as past inhabitants, if not more. The 'irregular triangle' of Parson's Green, as Fulham's historian C. J. Fèret described it in 1900[1], is much used today. It was acquired in 1881 by the Metropolitan Board of Works[2] as a public open space, but from 1971 administered by what is now Hammersmith and Fulham Council[3]. It provides a pleasant 5-minute walk to Parson's Green Station from the New King's Road, as well as a space for dogs, children and adults to play, and for sunbathing in summer. Some of the surrounding buildings have stood the test of time, especially the 18th century houses now part of Lady Margaret School, and the row of houses, dated 1795, facing the Green on the New King's Road. St Dionis' church and 'The White Horse' pub are landmark reminders of the 19th century.

This booklet takes a walk round the Green, sketching the history of its appearance and the buildings bordering it now, as well as some of their interesting past inhabitants. Many of the buildings had extensive grounds and gardens behind them, until they were built over in the housing boom of the 1880s and 1890s, which determined how the Green still looks today. The name 'Parson's Green' sometimes refers to an area wider than just the houses round the Green, but we have space only to mention that wider area in an Epilogue.

---

1 *Fulham Old and New, Volume 2*. Charles James Fèret (1854-1921) was the editor of the Fulham Chronicle, and worked on his 3-volume history of Fulham for over 10 years. The present work quotes extensively from this important book, hereafter referred to as Fèret. We do not identify him as our source every time, but if in doubt, assume it is him. Like him, we hold resolutely to the apostrophe in Parson's, despite modern disregard. 'Parsons Green' would mean something quite different: a club for naïve or environmentally concerned clergy perhaps!

2 The MBW was the main governing body for the whole of London from 1855 till the formation of the London County Council in 1889. They paid £5,000 for Parson's Green, Eelbrook Common and Brook Green.

3 Fulham became part of the London Borough of Hammersmith in 1965. The Council changed the name in 1979 to Hammersmith and Fulham, reacting to public feeling in Fulham that their historic name should not be lost.

The Green ...

The Domesday Book described the area as agricultural and pastoral, rich in woodland and capable of supporting large numbers of pigs - later, in 1476, Alice Parker was in trouble when her pig was a 'common nuisance' on the Green! The origin of the Green can be traced back to medieval times when people built houses round the 'village' green, where there was a pond for animals to use. The pond was fed by a natural spring from time immemorial; this made it a natural centre for habitation, and traces have been found of a prehistoric settlement in the garden of Lady Margaret School a few yards to the north[4]. On the west side of the Green a clump of trees was known as Parson's Grove as early as 1424. But it is not until John Bowack's *The Antiquities of Middlesex* of 1705[5] that we get a clearer picture of the Green. He describes it as a place 'inhabited mostly by Gentry and Persons of Quality' who lived in 'several very handsome houses, all standing very Airy upon a dry, clean green'.

John Norden, writing in 1593, said that the soil of Middlesex was 'excellent fat and fertile', but he regretted that there were so many country seats owned by citizens of London whose properties were ornamental rather than cultivated for arable crops for the London market. This had changed by the 18th century. The land to the west of London was covered in market gardens supplying fruit and vegetables to the capital.[6] The sale of one such was at Parson's Green in 1787[7], belonging to Messrs Rough and

---

4 See page 30.

5 John Bowack lived in Chelsea in 1705-6, and had several jobs including writing master at Westminster School; he was also an antiquarian. In 1732 he was Clerk to the Commissioners of Turnpike Roads; and in 1737 Assistant Secretary to the Westminster Bridge Commissioners at £100p.a. (*Dictionary of National Biography [DNB]*). Fèret says he lived in Sands End Lane from 1730-56.

6 Map 2 on page 69 shows a wide extent of market gardens in the immediate area still in 1865.

7 Contemporary press cutting.

Maynard. It included a house, stables and other buildings with 15 acres of land, 2,000 fruit trees, 8,000 gooseberry and currant bushes. Also for sale were 'a great quantity of feeds, 2 horses, 2 carts and other effects'; quite apart from 'The growing crop of vegetables to be taken by the purchaser of the lease at a fair valuation'. A market garden of this size was typical and could have been anywhere near the Green. 'The flourishing market gardens made Fulham a prosperous place, especially from about the 1750s until the 1850s.'[8] Many people were employed in the market gardens, especially in the summer. Women came from as far afield as Wales to pick strawberries; they transported them to Covent Garden in baskets on their heads so that the fruit would arrive fresh and undamaged.

According to Fèret the population of Parson's Green was about 80 in 1625, which grew to 360 in 1674. By 1739 it had dropped again to about 225, presumably because there were more market gardens, and fewer but larger houses inhabited by wealthier people.[9] The Green was in its heyday in the 18th century: 'Parson's Green remained a favourite locality for people of means. A number of substantial new houses were built around the Green during the 18th Century'[10].

But 'the 19th Century saw the development of Fulham from a riverside village with a hinterland of market gardens into a suburb of London' [11], though as late as 1872 Kelly's Post Office Directory listed some residents of Parson's Green Lane and Peterborough Road as cowkeepers. The building boom at the end of the century displaced the market gardens. Parson's Green Station was built in 1880 as part of the Metropolitan District Railway. James Thorne wrote in 1876[12] that Parson's Green was 'a century ago a very favourite place of abode' but now 'several of the best houses have indeed been pulled down or altered and others are empty and half-ruinous, but some remain, the Green is still verdant and the Elms vigorous'. Elms

---

8 Hasker, *Hammersmith and Fulham through 1500 Years*. Fuller details of the main works consulted and quoted are in the Bibliography on page 73.

9 Map 1 on page 68 shows the area in 1741-45.

10 Hasker, *op. cit.*

11 Winnett, *St Dionis' Parson's Green:The Second 50 Years.*

12 Thorne, *Handbook to the Environs of London.*

were always a feature of the Green from the earliest times. Fèret records that in 1456 Agnes Hasele was in court because she had cut down part of two trees without permission of the Lord of the Manor – the Bishop of London. Part of what is now Lady Margaret School was named The Elms (later Elm House) because of the trees in front of it[13], but sadly there are no elms today. They have been replaced with the ubiquitous London planes; probably, from the size of them, in the early 1900s.

Parson's Green Rectory house in the 18th and 19th centuries

... And its Parson

Back in 1705 Bowack wrote, 'Before the said house [the Parsonage or Rectory House] is a large Common which, within the memory of several ancient inhabitants now living, was used for a Bowling Green belonging to the said Rector, and served for his own and his domestiks' [sic] Diversion,

13 See page 26, and Map 2 on page 69. There was also High Elms House at nearby Purser's Cross (page 61).

from whence 'tis most likely the place was call'd Parson's Green'. The area was owned by the Bishop of London as Lord of the Manor. Fulham had been granted to Erconwald, Bishop of London, in *c.* 691. The earliest allusion to the Rectory house was in 1401 when the lands were farmed by Carthusian monks in Sheen. The first Rector of Fulham is recorded as far back as 1242, and the early ones may have lived in the Rectory. But the post was always a sinecure, that is, the Rector had another job at a church or churches elsewhere and just collected the tithes from the land attached to the parsonage. As Canon A.R. Winnett, the historian of today's St Dionis' church's first century[14], comments: 'The rectory of Fulham was a sinecure and involved no duties beyond appointing the Vicar of Fulham and providing a bull and boar for increasing the livestock of the parish'. Therefore for most of its existence the Rector of Fulham didn't live there but leased the house to tenants.

The Vicar of Fulham, based at All Saints' near Putney Bridge, was the one who actually had the cure of souls and did the work (though even some of them held more than one post!). Mention of them can be found from the 14th century onwards.[15] The last Rector, the Rev. William Wood, held the post from 1811 till his death in 1841. But he was made Vicar at the same time, and the two posts were effectively amalgamated. He bought the Rectory on Parson's Green and leased the tithes to members of his family. When the last one died in 1881, the tithes were taken over by the Ecclesiastical Commission which had been formed in 1835 to rectify abuses in the Church of England, such as sinecures.

14 Winnett, *op.cit.* The Rev. Canon Dr Winnett belonged to the church as a young person, before being ordained and serving in parishes in the Guildford diocese. Even though the church itself no longer does so, we pedantically follow Winnett in including the apostrophe at the end of the church's name; it is the church of, or dedicated to, St Dionis. St Dionis Road (see page 19) has no apostrophe, but road name-plates tend to be a lost cause!

15 For a full list of Rectors and Vicars of Fulham see Fèret, Volume 2. In 1758 a visitor to the area mentions the All Saints' vicarage as a red brick house with orchards and garden. The Rev. William Wood in 1812 and the Rev. Robert Baker in 1834 made alterations to the building.

The original Fulham parish was large and covered the whole of Fulham and Hammersmith, an area now densely populated and divided into several parishes. It stretched from the boundaries of Kensington and Chelsea on the east and Acton and Chiswick on the west, with the Thames to the south. Bowack wrote of Hammersmith in 1705, a mile to the north, that 'For about a hundred years past [it] has been a summer retreat for the nobility and wealthy citizens.' It had a 'chapel-of-ease', built in 1630-31; this was a subordinate church built within a parish to enable people to get to one nearer where they lived.[16] Until Hammersmith became a separate parish in 1834, the only parish church was Fulham's All Saints'.

Bowack mentions other villages near Parson's Green that were also part of the parish. There was Walham Green to the north-east, inhabited mainly by gardeners supplying Westminster and Covent Garden markets daily; 'here', he writes, 'are no houses of any considerable note'. North End he describes as a 'pleasant airy village inhabited mostly by gardeners'. Broom-house [sic] was part of Sands End, where there was a workhouse employing 70 or 80 people making sailcloth.

16 Information from the St Paul's Hammersmith leaflet, *The Meaning and History of the Church Building*. The present St Paul's on Hammersmith Broadway was built in 1883.

The Pond and Drinking Fountain

There was a pond in the south-east corner of the Green, known in the 17th century as Colepitts. It gradually became dirty and used only by dogs, ducks and market gardeners' horses; though according to those Fèret spoke to with long memories, village boys used to bathe there. Tradition had it that it was deep enough for Baptists to use it for baptism by immersion. It was drained and filled in in 1870, when the mains drainage was completed along New King's Road and replaced the spring.

The Rev. Robert Baker, who was Vicar of All Saints' for 37 years, retired to Parson's Green in 1871.[17] Shortly before he died in 1878, he paid for a handsome polished granite drinking fountain to be erected on the south side of the Green, near where the pond had been.

A glimpse of Parson's Green with the drinking fountain, 1916

17 See p. 64.

Sport

Apart from the Rector's bowling green already mentioned[18], the Green has hosted other sports. Fulham Football Club played on the ground for two years from 1889; they moved to their present ground only in 1896. The Rev. Shaun Atkins' family and friends played a game of hockey on the Green on Boxing Day each year while he was the previous Vicar of St Dionis' (1991-2004).

But the game with the longest association is cricket; the Green was a venue for cricket matches for well over 100 years. There were two matches there between Fulham and Chelsea, in 1731 and 1733.[19] They played for the substantial sum of 30 guineas (over £7,000 today)[20]. Fulham won both games, the second by the narrow margin of 3 runs. The same teams had played earlier in 1731 on Chelsea Common; and Fulham had played Putney at Putney Heath in 1730.

Fulham went on to great things and grander venues, culminating in 1907. That season star batsman H.W. Frampton scored 183 against Hammersmith, 109 not out against Cane Hill, and 101 not out against Hounslow. But he was not alone: in the last match of which we have a record, on 11 Sept. 1907 against Cross Arrows (the MCC staff cricket club) at Lord's, his opening partner F.R. Holmes scored 202 not out in Fulham's winning total of 319 for 1 wicket declared. The scorecard was listed in full in the publication *Cricket: A Weekly Record of the Game* because 'an individual score of over 200' was deemed 'of sufficient rarity at headquarters to warrant the full score being given'.[21] This great achievement seems to have been a case of

---

18 See p. 10.

19 *Wikipedia*.

20 https://www.in2013dollars.com/UK-inflation#formulas.

21 We are grateful to Robert Curphey of MCC's library at Lord's Cricket Ground, and to Rohan Kapadia of today's Fulham Cricket Club, for the information in this paragraph.

leaving the best till nearly last, as there are no further records of cricket in Fulham from 1912 onwards. Like so many other things, it appears to have perished with the Great War.

Although the reports we have traced refer to the team simply as Fulham, we assume it was the same as the 'Fulham Albion Cricket Club' which was based at 'The White Horse' on Parson's Green[22]. We have not been able to trace the origin of 'Albion' in its name, unless it is some connection with Albion House[23], two doors down from 'The White Horse'. Fèret described it as 'the pioneer cricket club in Fulham'. The early years of the 20th century saw a flowering of cricket in the area, with other teams called Parson's Green, Walham Green and Fulham Tradesmen. Parson's Green was the strongest, with its 2nd XI frequently beating the other clubs' 1sts.[24] The 21st century Fulham Cricket Club, based in South Park, is consciously trying to revive this rich heritage, with coaching and courses for children and over-60s.[25]

Women's cricket has come to prominence in recent years, but it is not a new development. In 1835 *The Times* reported on what it called a 'Singular Cricket Match' for women on Parson's Green: 'A vast assemblage of persons were congregated to witness the sport, amongst whom were a number of most respectable inhabitants'. The match was between Married Women in light blue and Single Women in white 'with pink sashes and cap-bows'. The Single Women won by 7 runs. After the match there was country dancing to a band with supper provided by 'The White Horse'.

---

22 Denny, *A History of Fulham*

23 See page 27. Has Denny possibly confused 'The White Horse' with its next-door-but-one 'The White House' (as Albion House was popularly known, see page 34)? It was a common and understandable mistake. The suggestion that the Cricket Club's 'Albion' may have been in imitation of West Bromwich Albion football club, which changed the third word in its title from 'Strollers' in 1879-80, is less likely, as 'Albion' was a district of West Bromwich where some of the players lived and worked (*Wikipedia*).

24 We assume this was the team representing the Parson's Green Working Men's Club from 1885. Despite the name, their playing field was a little further south on Mr Bell's field, adjoining Broomhouse Lane (see page 21).

25 See fulhamcricketclub.com.

Parson's Green Fair

Parson's Green Fair, painted by Thomas Rowlandson (1756-1827)

The Fair was established in the reign of William III (1689-1702) and took place on three days in August. A Mr C. Griffin wrote about 'Parson's Green in Olden Times' in the parish magazine in 1884: there were the 'usual concomitants of an ancient country fair, such as greasy pole climbing, treacle bobbing, ale-broaching and competitive hot tea drinking'. 'Honest' John Phelps who remembered the fair described it: 'My mother sold oysters there ... the canvas booths were all ranged about under the trees, where they sold gingerbread and such like commodities ... It was a wonderful nice fair but I remember one thing that wasn't nice. Poor live cocks used to be tied up by their legs and people threw sticks at them'. 'Along the King's Road side, it was general custom to arrange puppet shows and acting booths. On the West side were refreshment stalls. At the top of the Green, near 'The White Horse' were the fish stalls, oysters & whelks always being in demand. In the early years of this century [i.e. the19th] 'Billy' Button, a noted clown, used to ride his horse at the fair. After going through its antics, the intelligent animal would throw its rider off and 'bolt' for the stables of 'The White Horse'. In 1823 the Fair was suppressed by the magistrates'. Presumably it was getting a bad reputation.

Today there is an annual fair on the Green on the first Saturday in July. It was started by people from St Dionis' church in the 1990s and is now organised by Fulham Good Neighbours, a charity that provides help for older members of the community, 'working towards a community where neighbours look out and care for each other'[26]. At other times, travelling fairground entertainments for children come for a few days.

26 www.fulhamgoodneighbours.org.

West Side
(proceeding south to north)

The Vicarage

We approach St Dionis' Vicarage, No. 18 Parson's Green, via the late 19th century row of houses, Nos. 20-36[27]. They were built in 1888, and eight of them were inhabited in time for that year's electoral register. Before numbers became standard, they were given names in alphabetical sequence from the north: Algarve, Bancroft, Claremont, Delamere, Fairlawn, Grovedale, Holmewood and Ingleville; No. 28, which would have had a name beginning with E, was evidently still unoccupied. The names have all disappeared; and the one house (No. 36) which still displays one has changed it to 'Greenway'.

The medieval Rectory had many tenants. One was Sir William Butts, physician to Henry VIII. He was painted by Holbein and died in 1545, being buried in All Saints'. Another, from 1590, was Ursula, Lady Walsingham, widow of Sir Francis, Elizabeth I's Principal Secretary and 'spymaster'. The old house was demolished in stages between 1707 and 1740, and rebuilt as a square, red brick house about which Fèret comments that the rooms 'were

Sir William Butts, physician to King Henry VIII. Portrait by Hans Holbein.

27 On this side of the Green there are even house numbers only (numbered from north to south; odd numbers are on the east side.

mostly dark and small, hardly suggestive of affording any large amount of comfort'. This house was in turn demolished in 1882 to make way for St Dionis' church in 1885 and today's Vicarage, the final commission of the architect William White, in 1898-9. It is Grade II listed.

It found an enthralled occupant in Anne Atkins, the novelist and broadcaster, and wife of St Dionis' previous Vicar: 'When I first biked past it, I suppose in 1990, I fell in love ... Yes, as if with a person; as suddenly and completely. And yes, the Vicarage became a member of our family too; the heart of it. I miss the doorbell going all day long. … I miss Tony – most perhaps. He slept under Putney Bridge, and came for breakfast. Or lunch, or tea. In the snow and rain and sun. We sat on the Vicarage doorstep, under the magnolia I planted small that now spreads in the sky, a plate of bacon and eggs on his knee and a big mug of tea for each of us, and I asked him how one ends on the streets. "Something happens; I lost my partner; your heart breaks." … We left the Vicarage. We left Tony. (I wonder who feeds him now?) And my heart broke, I suppose.'

St Dionis' Church

There was originally no church on the site, only the Rectory or Parsonage with a chapel attached to it. But Canon Winnett mentions Fulham's 19th century transformation into a London suburb, 'for whose incoming population new churches had to be provided.'[28]

Charlotte Sulivan, a considerable heiress who lived nearby in Broom House, owned much of south Fulham at this time.[29] In 1876 she gave some land on which to build a Mission Hall in memory of her father Laurence Sulivan.[30] Designed by Arthur Billing, this stands today across St Dionis Road from the church, and is Grade II listed. The building cost £4,000 and could seat 300 people. It was to house services until a church could be built,

28 *Op. cit.*

29 See Sue Pierson, *Charlotte Sulivan*. Broom House was one of the great Fulham riverside mansions, at the end of Broomhouse Lane. It was demolished in 1911when the Hurlingham Club bought the estate.

30 The Mission Hall is still called that today. It has since been converted into two halls, one above the other, with proposals now for a third in the basement.

which it was in 1884-5, though the tower took another 11 years to complete. It was designed by Ewan Christian, who also designed the National Portrait Gallery. The church was mainly funded by the sale of Wren's St Dionis Backchurch in the City, which had been demolished in 1878; its communion table and plate, font and pulpit (designed by Grinling Gibbons) were given to the new church. But the bells, although granted to St Dionis' by an Order in Council, never arrived: they were moved temporarily to All Hallows', Lombard Street, but when it was demolished in 1937, its tower was reconstructed , complete with the bells, as part of All Hallows' Church, Twickenham, on the A316 Richmond Bypass / Great Chertsey Road. Having lost patience in 1899, the Ecclesiastical Commissioners gave St Dionis' a single bell (which is all the church ever had) from St Michael's, Bassishaw , which was about to be demolished on land now occupied by the Barbican Centre.[31] St Dionis has been identified as either Dionysius, the Athenian convert of St Paul in the New Testament[32], or Denys, Bishop of Paris in the 3rd century and patron saint of France. Winnett suggests that early legends confused and combined the two.[33]

In 1878 the Vicar of Fulham, the Rev. F.H. Fisher, put his curate, the Rev. John Stewart Sinclair, in charge of St Dionis'. In 1893 Sinclair wrote in the new St Dionis' magazine about the changes in the last 15 years: 'The 2,000 inhabitants had become 9,000 ... part of Fulham Road was a lane and New King's Road an avenue of trees' and 'the great Fulham oak was not yet replaced by Cortayne Road and the famous cedar still shaded the ground where a couple of hundred people live in Irene Road'.[34]

On 20 June 1897 there was a special service to honour Queen Victoria's Diamond Jubilee. The Bishop of Albany, USA, in his sermon described her

---

31 Information in this paragraph from Winnett, *A History of St Dionis'*. An 'Order in Council' is an instruction from the monarch on the advice of the Privy Council, a group of senior Government ministers who deal with some interdepartmental business through this forum.

32 Acts of the Apostles chapter 17: verse 34.

33 *St Dionis' ... The second 50 years.*

34 As Irene Road intersects with Delvino, this is presumably the tree in the grounds of Hollybush House recorded by Fèret. See page 40.

as a 'golden vessel and a vessel to honour. Her warm heart, her deep powers of sympathy, her world-wide influence have all been used for good'.

It took time to pay off the debt on the additional expense of building the tower.[35] In 1899 'A Grand Illuminated Fête and Sale of Work' was held in the grounds of Peterborough House.[36] The stalls included 'Fancy Work and Useful Articles', 'Cave for Fortune Telling' and 'Brantub, Cigar and Cigarette Stall'. It was estimated that 2,000 people attended and £141 was raised. After expenses had been paid, £74 was for the Tower Fund and £47 for 'special church expenses'.

The new Vicar, Dr W.S. Carter, was living at 23 Whittingstall Road off Fulham Road until the new Vicarage next to the church was completed later that year. He was Vicar for 32 years, from 1898-1931. He had had some legal training and could not let minor differences rest; they became major issues. On his death, the *Fulham Chronicle* said, 'He was a man of marked individuality and very definite opinions but he bore no ill-will to those who disagreed with him'.

Charlotte Sulivan died in 1911, leaving money to augment the Vicar's salary and for the upkeep of the Mission Hall. She bequeathed the house next to the Mission Hall (No. 16 Parson's Green) and, a little further north, the Ray of Hope Coffee House and Parson's Green Club (No. 6, now Ensor House, comprising the YMCA Hostel and St Dionis' Sulivan Hall, rebuilt in 1971 with flats above). She had started The Ray of Hope Coffee House in 1883 as an alternative attraction to local pubs. The Parson's Green Working Men's Club grew out of this and was officially formed in 1885 for respectable working men to 'discuss the topics of the day and combine instruction with amusement'[37]. They also played cricket in Mr Bell's field which bordered today's Bell's Alley, and is now occupied by Sulivan School.[38] When Charlotte Sulivan died, the Church Council, under Dr Carter, took over the Coffee House to use for church purposes: the club building was to be the

35 *Parson's Green, Fulham Parish Magazine.*
36 See page 48.
37 *Parson's Green, Fulham Parish Magazine.*
38 For the identity of Mr Bell, see page 64.

Parish House for church meetings. The members of the Club were outraged, as few of them were church members, and a bitter row ensued. Eventually the Hurlingham Club took over the cricket field and in its place gave the Club some land in Broomhouse Lane where they are to this day.[39]

In March 1918 Queen Alexandra and her daughter Princess Victoria were taken to see the design for the memorial screen in St Dionis' church. Her Majesty expressed her admiration for its beauty and elegance, and donated £2 towards the cost of £250. This doesn't sound particularly generous, but it would be worth at least £115 today.[40]

During the 8 years from 2012-20 the church building and grounds have undergone major refurbishment, seeking, in the words of current Vicar, the Rev. Tim Stilwell, 'to bring what felt like a 'tired' 19th century building bouncing back to renewed life in the 21st century. Our aim was to create more accessible space in a church with an obvious and inviting entrance on to Parson's Green, so that people can meet with God and each other, learn, teach, develop new skills and enjoy a quiet oasis in our fast-paced city.' The chief entrance between the Vicarage and the main church building is now visible to all who pass[41], unlike the old way in from St Dionis Road. Inside, the old tiled floor has given way to 450 sq. meters of natural oak parquet; movable chairs have replaced fixed pews; there are several small meeting spaces and a kitchen–café. The Royal Institute of British Architects chose to showcase the transformation in their 2021 London Awards.

St Dionis Road

St Dionis Road[42] originally rejoiced in the name of Muddy Lane! After that it was variously known from its connection with the earlier building on

---

39 For material in this paragraph, see Pierson, *op. cit.* The club's present premises were rebuilt to include flats in 2019. The original property and its legacy are now managed by the Charlotte Antonia Sulivan Charity.

40 https://www.in2013dollars.com/uk/inflation/1918.

41 It even announces its postal address, 18A Parson's Green. But the Mission Hall has no separate numbered address.

42 At the time of writing in mid-2021, the road has no name-plate at the Parson's Green end.

its corner as Rectory Road or Rectory (House) Lane; and there is still an old stone panel on No. 20 calling it Rectory *Place*. The name was officially changed to St Dionis Road in 1888 soon after the church was built; but locals still called it Rectory Road as late as 1914.[43] No. 2 is now converted to flats called Melbury Lodge, but is still visibly a former pub: 'The Jolly Brewers' was affectionately known to locals as 'Badbeers' and, perhaps as a result, closed in 2005. The row of houses from No. 6 to No. 70 is a terrace of 'Waterloo Cottages', built for soldiers returning from the Napoleonic Wars in the early 19th century. They are appreciably smaller than the later, Victorian houses opposite and beyond them.

Heathman's Road[44]

Shortly beyond the Mission Hall, next to No. 10 and 10A Parson's Green, is Heathman's Road, a narrow entrance to a small estate stretching to the railway line. It has some 25 random industrial and commercial units, including studios and even a vet's parlour. It seems a rare case of a road being named after its original inhabitants[45], J.H. Heathman & Co. They were makers of fire escapes and extinguishing appliances of all kinds, from fire engines and large ladders to the portable and throwable 'Swift' glass grenade full of chemicals supposed to douse the fire on impact[46]. Although they had other outlets in London as well and advertised their wares at Endell Street, W.C. as early as 1838, their factory and yard were at 10 Parson's Green from at least 1894 till at least 1929.[47] The house had been built in the mid-19th century, and is clearly older than the surrounding houses, with its quaint entrance up 8 steps to a round-headed door. It was

---

43 Loobey, *Hammersmith & Fulham Past & Present*. The road still appeared as Rectory Lane in *Stanford's Library Map of London and its Suburbs* in 1892.

44 3 cheers for the apostrophe on the road's name-plate - not that any of the occupants use it for their address!

45 Heathman's Road is not included in Velvick and Willson, *Street Names of Fulham and Hammersmith*.

46 After 40 years of use, the grenades were abandoned as ineffective.

47 *Internet*. Although the Ordnance Survey map of 1894-96 does not show them as such, they displayed their Telescopic Ladder Tower at the Royal Agricultural Show in June 1894, advertising their Parson's Green address.

renovated in 1976; today the house is two flats, with this visible upper entrance numbered 10A.

Advertisement for Heathman & Co. of Parson's Green, 1911

Rosamonds

Writing in 1900, Fèret says that No. 10 Parson's Green used to be called Rosamond Place as part of the Manor of Rosamonds. This historic Manor, named after a family called Rosemont or Rosemond in the 15th century, originally stretched from the old Rectory to Fulham Road. The resident of No. 10 in the 1870s, William Wainwright, was the brother of Henry Wainwright, hanged for the murder of Harriet Lane at Whitechapel in 1874. This notoriety led the next owner to change the house's name to Ash House Cottage. By the time of Heathman's 20 years later, it appears to have no name, merely the number.

The name 'Rosamonds' sometimes applied to the large estate, sometimes to the manor house itself, which stood behind where the YMCA building is today. Between the 15th and 17th centuries it developed from a 'tenement' (a building and portion of land, sometimes rented rather than owned) to a working farm and then a gentleman's residence.[48] By Fèret's time it had been divided into three dwellings, one known as Rosamond Cottage, and another at one stage as 'Rosamonds Dairy'[49]; the whole was finally demolished in 1926. It was then re-built, still with the name Rosamonds, as six flats by the Fulham Housing Improvement Society and opened by the Mayor in 1930. The *Fulham Chronicle* reported that they had been created to try to solve 'the local housing problem ... Needless to say, they could have been let over and over again'. The rent was 16/- a week, or 13/6 for the smaller flats. Photographs taken the following year show the visit of the Garden Cities and Town Planning Association[50]. The building was taken over in the 1970s by Octavia Housing, who built a further five flats in Lavinia House which borders the pavement. [51] Today this heir of the large medieval manor is overlooked and dwarfed by more recent developments.

---

48 We owe this overview of Rosamonds' history to P.D. Whitting in *A History of Hammersmith.*

49 It is a pleasant coincidence that the modern Dairy Close development is on virtually the same site. Before it was built there was a milk distribution centre there.

50 Now known as the Town and Country Planning Association, it was founded by Sir Ebenezer Howard in 1899, with the narrower aim of pioneering Garden Cities.

51 Rosamonds is now No. 2 Parson's Green and Lavinia House No. 4, marking the northern extent of the Green itself. Lavinia seems to have been the name of the eldest daughter of Helena Sinnott who bought the property from Charlotte Sulivan in 1900. Octavia Housing – named after Octavia Hill, the social housing reformer, who co-founded the National Trust – is a not-for-profit organization providing people with affordable homes in inner London.

Rosamonds today, No. 2 Parson's Green, photographed c. 1931

The name Rosamonds confusingly attached itself to other houses nearby. Thomas Crofton Croker (1798-1854) lived from 1837-46 in a house on the estate but the other side of Parson's Green Lane. Built in 1762, its name had been Brunswick Cottage, but Croker changed it to what Fèret called 'the fantastic designation of Rosamond's Bower'. Croker perpetuated the myth that the fair Rosamund, the mistress of Henry II, had lived there but there is no evidence that she ever did. By Croker's time the house had grown from a Tudor cottage to a 10-room dwelling. It became a rendezvous for the literati of the day. Croker was born in Ireland and devoted much of his early life to collecting legends and songs from Ireland. The 1841 census records him as 40 years old with a wife Maryan and a son Dillon, aged 9. He wrote *A Walk from London to Fulham* in the 1850s, describing what he saw on the way. The next occupant renamed the house Audley Cottage, and it was demolished in 1892.

East Side
(proceeding north to south)

The White Horse[52]

'The White Horse' pub is on the site where there was a coaching inn since at least 1688. It was first mentioned in *The Spectator* in 1712, in relation to the Fair when ale-tapping, or broaching a new barrel, was an eagerly awaited event[53].

Its most noted host was John Wright who so severely chastised a boy known as 'the Giant' that he died; John Wright became known as Jack the Giant Killer. After that the landlords changed frequently. It had been rebuilt in 1770 and was built again in its current form in 1886 when it was a free house owned by the James family. The statue of the horse under its canopy is suitably prominent.

Today it is known as the 'Sloaney Pony' as most of its patrons are young adults who work in the City but live locally. By ancient tenure the pub owns part of the land in front of the building where the patrons can sit outside in all weathers. On warm summer evenings it is very popular, and they spill out on to the pavement and across the road to the Green.

The Parson's Green Health Centre[54]

The present NHS walk-in centre occupies the site of two houses used in the 1860s by the London Female Preventive and Reformatory Institution (LFPRI), to reform young female delinquents who were respectable but

52 The address of today's pub is 1-3 Parson's Green. It was clearly built originally as two houses.

53 See page 16 for more about the Fair.

54 Today's address is 5-7 Parson's Green. It is possible to sense where there have been two or even three entrances, though today there is only one for the public, in the centre.

friendless. The Institution was a 'Certified Reformatory' recognised by the courts as an alternative to prison for 'fallen and degraded' girls. There was room for 50 inmates to be trained for domestic service. Their uniform consisted of a stiff, starched dress with bibbed aprons and little pointed caps with streamers. The houses belonged to the philanthropist Dr Holt Yates. After he died in 1874, they were rebuilt as the Holt Yates Memorial Home, and in 1886 renamed the Jubilee Training Home in honour of Queen Victoria's Golden Jubilee. Before that, from 1813-28, the southern end of the site was part of the next-door Albion House School (see Henniker House below – the two sites had overlapping histories, and were originally in the 14th century called 'Stowtes Tenement' after the name of the owner).

Tea-time at the Holt Yates Memorial Home, c. 1880

A new building on the site – the work of local firm W.J. Marston & Son – became the Fulham Maternity Home in 1937.[55] It still bears the old

55 The LFPRI ceased operating at this point, but its vision has been carried on by what is now Catch 22, the social business working with the most vulnerable in society.

Borough of Fulham coat of arms[56] and motto ('Pro Civibus et Civitate' – For the Citizens and the State) above the entrance. At the opening in October that year, the Mayor of Fulham remarked that it was 30 years too late for him as, being a father of 15, he would have been a regular customer! It had 28 beds, designed to accommodate 400 confinements a year, a fifth of the borough's annual total. The three floors contained maternity and childcare clinics, a baby food dispensary, dental rooms, isolation wards and ultraviolet and infra-red treatment rooms. One mother who was treated there was quoted in the Fulham Chronicle: '14 days in the Home is as good as a holiday'.[57] During the war that followed almost immediately, part of the Home was used as a First Aid Post for civilian casualties.

Many people still living locally were born there. One of them writes, 'I was born in Parson's Green Maternity Home just before Christmas 1955. My mother had been in labour for three days when everything started going badly wrong. The senior doctor, who was at a Christmas function, received a message saying that the baby was dead and the mother in grave danger. To everyone's relief I was born alive and my mother survived. A few days later, when my mother regained consciousness, she told a nurse that she had dreamed that I was delivered by a man wearing a bow tie with a bandage around his head. The nurse said, "Oh my dear, that wasn't a dream. The doctor was in such a hurry to get to you that he skidded on ice and had to be bandaged up as he was running through the corridor." I don't know the name of this dedicated man but I will always be grateful to him.'

One young mother, after having her daughter there, became an auxiliary nurse in the Home in the 1960s. 'In those days it was not normal for fathers to be at the birth, but many wanted to. It was my job to notify

---

56 The coat of arms was granted in 1927, and paid for by Cllr F.H. Barber, proprietor of Barbers' Department Store. The shield shows crossed swords and mitre representing the Bishop of London whose residence was Fulham Palace, on a wavy background representing the Thames. The crest uses a city wall to signify municipal government and a Danish ship which came to Fulham in 879 AD. Some of these features were incorporated into the current coat of arms for the Borough of Hammersmith and Fulham when they merged in 1965.

57 Material in this paragraph from the firm's centenary booklet, *W.J. Marston and Son 1895-1995*.

them of the impending birth, but many missed it by minutes and were quite disgruntled.'

It became today's drop-in centre in 1968 when the maternity wards were transferred to the new Charing Cross Hospital in Fulham Palace Road. Since 2018 it has also housed the Lilyville NHS GP surgery, which had been on the corner of Lilyville and Fulham Roads from 1991.

Lady Margaret School[58]

Belfield House, 1895

58 Today's address is 9-15 Parson's Green. There are the three constituent houses (see below), Henniker (No. 9), Elm (No. 11) and Belfield (Nos. 13 and 15). It is possible to see where there has been a fourth entrance at the southern end of the additional block to the south of Belfield House, which protrudes as far as the pavement and was original to the school, as it appears in photographs of 1920 and is inscribed 'Church Secondary School for Girls ...'. There is an obvious blank where '... and Boys' has been removed. Some of the information in this section comes from the history of the school, "*... a particularly happy place*", and from the booklet *Celebrating our Centenary.*

Lady Margaret School started life in 1842 under another name, as a practice school for Whitelands Teacher Training College in Chelsea[59]. In 1917 the college wanted to extend its premises and use the school's building, which was therefore faced with closure. Enid Moberly Bell, one of the teachers, was explaining the predicament to the Bishop of Kensington, John Maud, at St Dionis' Vicarage, when Mrs Carter, the Vicar's wife, told them that ***Belfield House*** on the east side of Parson's Green was for sale with an acre of land for £2,250. The present school's histories make no mention of this, but the Ordnance Survey map of 1913 (Map 4 on page 71) reveals that the building had most recently been in educational use as an Industrial School[60]. 'MB', as she was known, wanted her own school and with the help of friends bought the building, founded the school and named it Lady Margaret[61], and became its first, legendary headmistress. She maintained that the opening was all due to prayer, and continued to demonstrate her faith by preparing the girls for Confirmation. She took her dog to school every day; he is on her lap in school and staff photos. And if she had to stay late, she would put two pennies in his mouth and send him off to board the 22 bus unaccompanied to go home to 7 Mallord Street, Chelsea. This fabulous story, sounding too good to be true, is told as sober fact in the school's *Celebrating our Centenary* booklet. We assume the bus conductors must have been primed!

---

59 Whitelands was founded in 1841, and was one of the first Higher Education Colleges to admit women. After some years in Southfields, it is now part of Roehampton University.

60 This was a recognized classification from the 1830s for pauper children who were orphaned or abandoned, or had parents in the workhouse. From the 1850s Certified Industrial Schools were set up for children found begging, homeless, or committing an offence; or whose parents could not control them. The 1876 Elementary Education Act set up Day Industrial Schools 'for those children whose education is neglected by their parents, or who are found wandering, or in bad company'; they provided 'industrial training, elementary education, and one or more meals a day, but not lodging'.

61 After Lady Margaret Beaufort (1441/3-1509), mother of King Henry VII. She is credited with founding Christ's College, Cambridge in 1505, and then St John's College, Cambridge, completed in 1511 after her death. She also endowed lectureships at Oxford, where the Victorian foundation Lady Margaret Hall (one of the first two Colleges for women in the University) is also named after her.

Miss Moberly Bell and her staff, c. 1920

The first term started in September with paint still wet on the walls, the science lab – converted from the house's derelict stables - unfinished, a large debt, and World War 1 still raging. The intake was 86 girls and 11 boys (but only girls after World War 2). The school was dedicated by Bishop Maud on St Michael's Day, 29 Sept. 1917, and formally opened by Princess Marie Louise (granddaughter of Queen Victoria) on 6 Dec. In June 1918 the pupils presented a pageant about the history of Belfield House and the School, at which Princess Christian (the third of Queen Victoria's daughters, and the mother of Marie Louise) was present.

200 girls were evacuated to Midhurst in Sussex in 1939, returning in 1943. The school building was in a sorry state, having been requisitioned by the local Auxiliary Fire Service (volunteer assistants to the Fire Brigade); it took a tough few years to restore it. In 1937 ***Elm House***, next door to the north, had been added, and ***Henniker House*** beyond it followed in 1951; both had previously been schools (see below). In 1953, at its formal opening,

Cast of the pageant telling the history of Belfield House, 6 June 1918

Henniker was re-named Moberly Bell House in honour of MB's 30 years as headmistress, though the name has since reverted to Henniker. In 1970 the appearance of the buildings was described thus: 'despite the growing shabbiness of their surroundings they still display something of the mild opulence that formerly characterised Parson's Green'.[62]

Today Lady Margaret is a Church of England secondary academy for 775 girls, which has been 'offering an outstanding education for over 100 years'. Its future was never secure as a smaller school with only enough girls for two forms entering each year. In 1996 it grew to three-form entry, and in 2014 to four. As the school expanded, a number of new buildings have been added in the gardens at the back, and a very modern glass entrance at the front, dating from 2014. In 1998 when a new teaching block was constructed, the remains of a post-medieval garden and evidence of a prehistoric settlement were revealed.

62 Whitting, ed. *A History of Fulham.*

Earlier Occupants

Henniker House

Henniker House was named by the London County Council in the 1930s in memory of Jane Livesey Henniker, the first woman member of the Fulham Board of Guardians[63]. In the late 19th century the Board used the building on the site to house pauper children. In the early 1700s its predecessor was Albion House, which was white[64], and often known as 'The White House' – not to be confused with 'The White Horse', two doors up the road[65]. From 1813 it was Albion House boys' boarding school till 1828, when the owner of nearby East End House, John Daniel[66], bought it and then demolished it in 1830. He had it rebuilt as Park House in 1841 by Thomas Cubitt the master builder[67]. According to Fèret, Daniel designed it with solid oak floors to last a thousand years; at least 800 to go!

Elm and Belfield Houses

There are records of joint-ownership of the site of these two houses back in the 14th century, when it was known as Hore's Tenement. They became separate properties only in the 17th century.

Sir John Vaughan

For several years at that time the tenant was Sir John Vaughan (1574/5-1634). He was a Welsh courtier who by successful 'networking'

---

63 The Board of Guardians in each area administered the Poor Law and Workhouses from 1835-1930. Its powers and responsibilities then passed to local and national government bodies.

64 This may have influenced its name. 'Albion' is thought to derive from Latin *albus*, meaning white. 'Albion' as a name for Britain or England is closely connected with the white cliffs of Dover.

65 They were easily confused. See the possible case in note 23.

66 See below, page 45.

67 Thomas Cubitt (1788-1855) was the first builder to employ all his own craftsmen. He is famous for Osborne House and part of Buckingham Palace, as well as Belgrave Square and areas in Bloomsbury.

achieved the position of 'Comptroller'[68] or Treasurer of the Prince of Wales's Household, when it was set up in 1616. This was the future Charles I (born in 1600), who became heir to the throne on the death of his brother Henry in 1612. Although the position earned Sir John the lucrative wage of £428 p.a., he estimated that the expenses of running the Household cost him £20,000 for which he was not recompensed. He fell from favour when Charles became King in 1625; but in 1628 he was created first Earl of Carbery, a barony on the south-west coast of Ireland, perhaps as compensation. Like many with Irish titles, he seems to have been an absentee landlord, as he lived out the rest of his life on the Vaughan estate in Wales.

In 1621, while living at Elm House, he played host for six weeks to Sir Francis Bacon, the disgraced Lord Chancellor. Bacon was charged with 23 counts of bribery and corruption. He was said to have received gifts from litigants; although this was the custom of the time, he admitted he had been lax and pleaded guilty. He spent a few days in the Tower and although he was fined £40,000, this was remitted by the King, who then gave permission for him 'to be and remain at Sir John Vaughan's house at Parson's Green', in order to settle personal affairs. Bacon said he welcomed the house's 'sweet air and loving usage [which] much revived my languishing spirits'[69]. But his reputation was tarnished and he was forced into 'retirement' on his country estate, Gorhambury near St Albans. The last few years of his life were spent in writing and study. He died of pneumonia, supposedly from carrying out an experiment on the effects of freezing meat in the snow.

William Rumbold (1613-1667)

He bought Hore's Tenement in 1665 and spent the last three years of his life at Parson's Green. He was a friend of the Mordaunts at Villa Carey, later to become Peterborough House[70]. When his wife died three months after him, Lord Mordaunt and others became guardians of their three

68 This is not the same word as 'controller'. Derived from medieval French for keeping a 'counter roll', it involved financial supervision.

69 Bacon's letter to Prince Charles, later Charles I.

70 See pages 48-51.

young daughters. He had entered the office of the 'Great Wardrobe'[71] at 16. As a Royalist he was a standard bearer to King Charles I, but escaped to Spain with his brother Henry. He returned disguised as a merchant after 'the late King's murder'[72], but actively plotted for Charles II's return, and was imprisoned in the Tower from 1655-8. Cromwell tried to get Henry to return by offers of 'enlargement' to William, 'but he was not a subject to be so wrought'. Henry remained in Spain where he became a consul for Charles II after the Restoration; meanwhile William was installed 'in the offices of Comptroller[73] of the Great Wardrobe and Surveyor General of the Customs'[74]. His tomb is in the chancel of All Saints', where Henry is also buried. Nearby Rumbold Road took its name 'probably after the Rumbold family who had an estate at Parson's Green in the 17th century'.[75]

Elm House, formerly The Elms

In 1729 *The Country Journal* described Elm House as 'a large convenient House, with an Orchard, well-planted Gardens, Stable, Coach-Houses, and Out-Houses, a Row of large Elms before the Gates, pleasantly situated on a very healthy Ground. The House is fit for either Courtier, Merchant, or large Boarding-School. Enquire at the House, near the White House on Parson's-Green, on Mondays, Wednesdays and Fridays'.

In the early 19th century it was rebuilt and did indeed become a school: first from 1803-11 run by the Rev. William Pearson for young gentlemen,

71 This was the repository for portable royal property, such as clothing, tapestries, furniture, armoury and other treasures, in storage when not in use at court. By Rumbold's time, it was a separate department of Government, in a building on the site of today's Wardrobe Place in the City.

72 Quotes from Henry, writing in *c.* 1674 and quoted by Fèret.

73 See footnote 74. This post involved financial supervision of the Wardrobe department's expenditure.

74 From medieval times, 'Customs' referred to the duties payable to the crown on import or export of goods (hence 'going through Customs' today). In 1643 Parliament established a Board of Customs under a parliamentary committee; this is what Rumbold managed after the Restoration. It was ratified as a permanent Government department in 1671, shortly after his death; it survived till 1909 when it became part of HM Customs and Excise, and then in 2006 HM Revenue and Customs.

75 Velvick and Willson, *Street Names of Fulham and Hammersmith.*

and then a Roman Catholic school under various owners until 1832. In the meantime the house had been bought in 1820 by John Daniel, intent on buying up the whole row; he let it as a single residence to tenants. In 1890 it returned to educational use as a School of Discipline for Girls; by the time of Map 4 on page 71 (1913) it had the gentler name of a 'Receiving Home', which cared temporarily for children with no homes of their own. In 1933 it changed its name again to Approved School for its last four years before becoming part of Lady Margaret.

Elm House, 1895

Belfield House

The oldest part of the house seems to have been built about 1650; today's front is early 18th century. John Daniel bought it as well as next-door Elm House in 1820, and from 1825-49 it was the residence of his nephew Thomas Daniel Belfield, recorded as a merchant in the 1841 census. The house took its name from him.

Mrs Jordan

Later local historians, quoting Fèret, have perpetuated the myth that Mrs Jordan, the mistress of the Duke of Clarence (later King William IV), lived here during their liaison from 1790-1811. There is no evidence for this, as she lived at Bushey Park with the ten children she bore the future King. Claire Tomalin, Mrs Jordan's biographer[76], confirmed to us in private correspondence that Belfield House's claim is an unfounded rumour. The story probably started because of a carved fireplace in the house, bearing the initials W and J, supposedly for 'William' and 'Jordan'. We think this highly unlikely, as lovers would have carved W and D for William and Dora[77]. It seems probable that she was confused with Mrs Fitzherbert, 'wife' of the Prince Regent (William's elder brother), who lived in next-door East End House during the same period.[78] If two royal mistresses were in fact living next door to each other at the same time, the evidence would surely be far stronger.

Theodore Roussel (1847-1926)

He bought the house in 1890 and did much-needed repair; he restored the handsome staircase and windows that had been blocked because of the earlier window tax. He was a self-taught artist who had achieved notoriety in 1887 by displaying his painting of 'The Reading Girl' at the New English Art Club. The 'Girl' is a life-size nude and is now in Tate Britain. At Parson's Green he painted atmospheric landscapes, usually featuring the Thames. The American-born but London-based artist James Abbott McNeill Whistler became a lifelong friend and mentor who introduced him to etching. One etching dated 1906 is 'Sign of the White

---

76 Tomalin, *Mrs Jordan's Profession*.

77 She was born Dorothea Bland in 1761, but usually known as Dora or Dorothy. She never married, and there was no Mr Jordan. She was an actress, and in common with many in her profession, she adopted the title and name as a badge of respectability. She died in 1816 before William became King.

78 See below, page 40.

Horse'.[79] His old studio became the school's Art Room, although it has since been built over.

'The Reading Girl' painted by Theodore Roussel

Roussel was a friend of Archibald Hartrick, the artist who lived in Clancarty Road in the house next to South Park. He moved there in 1908 and his house was described as 'the last house in London'. He learnt from locals that before South Park was created in 1903, the farm next to his house stretched down to the river, with fields, vegetables and fruit trees.[80]

79 It was obviously drawn from outside his house, and shows the pub and houses overshadowed by a large tree. Copies available from Harris Schrank Fine Prints (harrisschrank.com).

80 Hartrick, *A Painter's Pilgrimage through Fifty Years.*

Hollybush House – later East End House

Hollybush House (exterior) in the 19th century, sketched by one of John Daniel's daughters

The land from Lady Margaret to the New King's Road, today filled by the elaborate and modernised Victorian houses numbered 17-21, then Delvino Road[81] and the post-War blocks Nos. 23-41[82], was a single property, Hollybush House, overlooking the Colepitts pond on the Green[83]. Although Thorne called it 'a plain white house on the east side of the Green ... built by Sir Francis Child, Lord Mayor of London in 1699'[84], it had a longer history still. It was originally an Elizabethan house built and occupied by Sir William Billesbie, a senior civil servant under Elizabeth I and James I, who died in 1607/8. He sold it in 1606 to Sir Thomas Smith of Brightwells who

81 The road was laid down in 1880, four years before the demolition of East End House. S.L. Velvick and E.J. Willson, compilers of *Street Names of Fulham and Hammersmith*, do not know the origin of the name Delvino.

82 There was a row of 10 Victorian houses here, marked as 'damaged beyond repair' in the *LCC Bomb Damage Maps, 1939-45.*

83 See page 13.

84 *Op. cit.*

was an MP, Clerk to Parliament and Master of the Court of Requests.[85] The name Hollybush is explained in a court record of 1626 which calls it a place 'where elms and hollybushes grow'. It was later sold to Robert Blanchard who was a goldsmith and partner of Francis Child under the sign of 'Ye Marygold', which eventually became Child's Bank in Fleet Street. Blanchard died in 1681 and was buried in All Saints'; his wife Martha died in the house in 1685. Blanchard left £5 to the poor of Fulham for 'such as are old and have been sober, honest, laborious and frequenters of the church'[86]. He also left £1 p.a. 'to be distributed in bread on the Sunday after 10th June'[87].

Child inherited the estate, as he had become Martha's son-in-law on marrying her daughter Elizabeth by her first marriage. He was knighted by William III in 1689, and served as Lord Mayor for 1698-9. He improved and enlarged the house – rather than building it from scratch, as perhaps implied by Thorne above - to be what Fèret called 'a perfect specimen of what is known as Queen

Sir Francis Child with Lord Mayor's sword. Portrait by an unidentified artist.

85 The Court of Requests was a travelling royal court that settled disputes between royal servants, and heard cases brought by the poor. It dealt more speedily than the common law courts. There is further information about both Billesbie and Smith, including their memorials in All Saints', in Pierson, *Peterborough House*, pp. 7-10. The Brightwells estate stretched south of where the New King's Road is today.

86 His will, quoted by Fèret.

87 Lysons, *The Environs of London*.

Anne style of architecture'. It had 16 acres of grounds[88] including a rose garden, fruit garden and orangery. Just before his death in 1713, he bought Osterley Park[89], which his grandson Robert remodelled from 1763-80 with the foremost architect of the day, Robert Adam. Sir Francis left money to the poor of Fulham among others and is buried in All Saints' churchyard.

Bowack, describing the house in 1705, called it 'well-built with brick after the modern manner and looks very stately; the gardens also are very good'[90]. He also mentioned an adjoining property belonging to 'Mr Poultney, a Turkey merchant[91]; this is a large regular new built brick house and is made very convenient. There is also Twos or Threes[92] other very handsome seats here.'

Admiral Sir Charles Wager (1666-1743)

After Sir Francis Child's death, his son Robert inherited Hollybush. But in 1720 he leased it to the Admiral for 22 years. After 20 years at sea gathering fame and fortune, Wager now spent the rest of his life ashore. In the Wars of the Spanish Succession in 1708, he had been in command of four English ships which attacked a Spanish fleet of 17 galleons, and sank the flagship, which carried an estimated £7 million in gold and silver. Wager managed to save about £100,000 in prize money for himself. While living at Hollybush, he served as an MP and also remained a senior administrator of the Navy. He was what we call today the First Sea Lord from 1730-33, and then First Lord of the Admiralty from 1733-41.[93] He was

---

88 To give a comparison: modern Eelbrook Common nearby is about 14 acres.

89 Now in the care of the National Trust; see nationaltrustcollections.org.uk/place/osterley-park. It was built by Sir Thomas Gresham before 1576.

90 *Op. cit.*

91 A Turkey merchant was not a poultry seller, but a member of an English company which conducted trade with Turkey and the Levant. It was formed in 1581 and dissolved in 1825.

92 Sic! He presumably means 'There are also two or three other …'. He is perhaps referring to Albion, Elm and Belfield Houses in the same row along the east side of Parson's Green.

93 The First Lord of the Admiralty is the political head of the Navy, senior adviser to the Government on naval matters. The First Sea Lord and Chief of Naval Staff is the professional head of the Navy, as senior officer; in Wager's day, the post was called Senior Naval Lord to the Board of Admiralty.

'a one-man bureau of maritime intelligence'[94], with considerable administrative skills, and was generous and trusted. In Fulham he was the first chairman of subscribers to the Fulham Bridge Company[95]; and he cared for the Hollybush garden, where a noted magnolia grandiflora flowered in 1737. A year before his death he was pensioned off and was living at Stanley House in Chelsea. There is a monument to him in Westminster Abbey.

Sir Robert Child died without issue in 1721, and his brother, another Francis, inherited. He was unmarried, a banker and very rich, and died in 1740. Both brothers, like their father, are buried at All Saints'. Hollybush was inherited by yet another brother, Samuel Child.

Admiral Sir Charles Wager. Portrait by Thomas Gibson.

John Powell

Samuel eventually sold the house in 1752 to John Powell, who modernised it and renamed it East End House, fitting its position at the south-east corner of Parson's Green. When what is now known as the eastern arm of Parson's Green was first laid down as a through road, its name was East End Road[96], presumably taken from the house it bordered. Of the house Fèret says , 'It was of red brick. The front door was solid mahogany. The inner doors, panelling, floors, staircases and shutters were of oak.' Powell and his family became principal landowners in the area;

94 *DNB.*
95 Fulham Bridge (1729-1886) was the precursor of today's Putney Bridge, and slightly down-river to the north of it.
96 See Map 4 on page 71.

in 1773 he agreed to invest £114.3.0 in return for permission to enclose a portion of waste land in the parish (it is not known where). The dividends were shared equally between the poor of Fulham and Hammersmith; in Fulham the money was spent on providing bread and beef.[97]

It is hard to trace exactly when Powell lived at East End House, as opposed to letting it out to tenants; but it seems he was in residence from 1778 till he died in 1784. Various tenants followed.

Mrs Fitzherbert (1756-1837)

Mrs Fitzherbert, the 'secret wife' of the Prince Regent (later King George IV), was the tenant from 1808-10. She altered the house considerably and improved the garden. Born Maria Anna Smythe in 1756, she was married to the Prince of Wales in 1785; she had already been widowed twice. She was a great beauty and was painted by Sir Joshua Reynolds. She was a Roman Catholic and the King, George III, had not given his consent. The marriage was declared invalid under English Civil Law. The Prince Regent had run up enormous debts which Parliament would only pay off if he produced a legal heir. Mrs Fitzherbert was reduced to the status of mistress in 1795, when he married his cousin Caroline of Brunswick. She was short, fat, ugly and smelly. The marriage was not a success, but they managed to produce Princess Charlotte! George tried to divorce Caroline, but she went to live abroad. When he became King in 1820 the government offered her £50,000 to stay out of the country, but she refused and came to live in Hammersmith - hence Queen Caroline Street, W6. The Prince, now George IV, refused to let her into Westminster Abbey for the coronation. When he died in 1830 he left all his 'worldly property ... to' Mrs Fitzherbert, 'the wife of my heart and soul'[98].

---

97 Information from anonymous and undated leaflet entitled *Fulham United Charities*. In 1880 the Powell fund and 20 other charities were amalgamated into these Fulham United Charities. In 1999 this was wound up and capital grants were distributed to local schools; the maintenance of memorials and churchyards; the music and organ at All Saints'; and a Vicar's Discretionary Fund. There is a plaque commemorating these changes in the north porch of All Saints'.
98 *Wikipedia*.

Mrs Fitzherbert. Portrait by Sir Joshua Reynolds.

John Daniel

In 1814 East End House was bought by John Daniel, remembered by Fèret as 'Squire' Daniel. He was a wealthy West India merchant and slave owner, with properties in Antigua, Barbados, British Guiana, Montserrat, Nevis and Tobago. He was a partner in the firm of Thomas Daniel and Sons which was one of the largest single recipients of slave compensation, notably from Barbados and British Guiana.[99] He continued to live in East End House, despite buying and developing the neighbouring houses, Belfield, Elm and Albion. The 1841 census records him at 73 with daughters Eleanor (33), Mary (31) and Anne (29). Ten years later at 83 he is living with Eleanor, Anne and her daughter Sybella, who was a widow. They were

99 *Internet.*

served by a butler, housemaids, lady's maids, a cook, gardener, coachman and carpenter. John died in 1853 and was buried at All Saints' along with several of his family. Eleanor Daniel, aged 76, laid the foundation stone of St Dionis' church in 1884.

In 1864 the house was sold to Mr Grant Heatly Tod-Heatly, the last occupant. On one occasion he entertained the Prince of Wales there, the future King Edward VII. When the house was demolished in 1884, the trees were cut down including a veteran cedar, about 150 years old, which had to be blown up with gunpowder. It was 'of remarkable growth – the branches descend to the ground in every direction and their whole circumference is about 120 feet'[100].

East End House (interior), painted by one of John Daniel's daughters

100 Faulkner, *An Historical and Topographical Account of Fulham*, written 70 years earlier in 1813.

South Side
(proceeding east to west)

New King's Road[101]

The King's Road was originally a farm track, widened in Stuart times as a private road for the Kings to travel by coach from St James's or Whitehall palaces to the ferry at Fulham, and thence by boat to Hampton Court. Pedestrians could use the road without restriction, but from 1731 the owners of carts and carriages were required to have passes to get through the four gates in Chelsea and two in Fulham. The passes were bronze or copper discs, with the royal cipher on one side and 'THE KING'S PRIVATE ROADS'[102] on the other. New issues were made to address the growing

Parson's Green south side with New King's Road, c. 1905

101 We are indebted to James Sproule, who has researched the history of his house in New King's Road, for information in this section, and those on 'Duke on the Green' and Pitt Place, which follow.
102 Sic: both the capital letters and the plural 'ROADS'. The King owned other roads as well.

prevalence of forgeries. Traffic must have been considerable, as 25 nursery gardening firms are known along the road from 1750 to 1916. It became a public road only in 1830. In 1865 it was upgraded, and the stretch from Bagley's Lane to Putney Bridge was renamed New King's Road.

It was along New King's Road that the 21-year-old Oxford undergraduate John Betjeman claimed to have driven with friends 'in a damn'd old lorry' from Putney to Trafalgar Square as part of a student prank; 'And I saw a bobby at Parson's Green who looked like running us in.'[103]

Peterborough House[104]

Villa Carey, later known as Peterborough House

By far the most impressive house and grounds at Parson's Green was Peterborough House, on the southern edge of the Green and south of New King's Road. Its origins went back to medieval times but it came into its own in the reign of Charles I, when the Carey family owned it and called it Villa

103 'The 'Varsity Students' Rag', first published in Cherwell magazine, 29/10/1927. Now in John Betjeman's *Collected Poems*, John Murray, 1958 / 2006, p.5.
104 See fuller treatment with references in Pierson, *Peterborough House*.

Carey. John Mordaunt, son of the first Earl of Peterborough[105], married Elizabeth Carey in 1657. He supported Charles II in exile and coming to the attention of Cromwell in 1658, he was imprisoned in the Tower. He was eventually released 'by judicious bribery and blind luck'[106]. He was headstrong and impatient, unlike his wife who John Evelyn the diarist called 'the most virtuous lady in the world'. Mordaunt was a keen gardener, and showed Evelyn how to make a hot-bed[107] and impressed him with his knowledge of horticulture.[108] Mordaunt died in1675, aged 49. His heroic statue can be seen under the tower in All Saints'.

Charles Mordaunt, Third Earl of Peterborough, 1715. Portrait by Sir Godfrey Kneller.

Their son Charles, the third Earl of Peterborough, changed the name to Peterborough House. He had a distinguished military career and was instrumental in putting William of Orange on the throne, but 'he seems

105 John was never Earl himself. The title passed to the first Earl's brother and then to John's son.
106 *DNB*.
107 In horticulture a hotbed (now without the hyphen) is a bed of earth heated by fermenting manure, for raising or forcing young plants. This led to the figurative use of the word to mean an environment for speeding the growth of something, usually unwelcome, eg 'hotbed of vice' (*Concise Oxford Dictionary [COD]*).
108 John Evelyn's diary, quoted in Denny, *op. cit.* Evelyn (1620-1706) wrote a diary for over 50 years commenting on art, culture and politics. He was well known for his knowledge about trees.

to have been a petulant, childish and vainglorious character'[109]. In 1705, Bowack wrote: 'This seat is a very large square, regular pile of brick and has a gallery all round it upon the roof. It has abundance of extraordinary good rooms with fine paintings etc., but is most remarkable for its spacious gardens, there being 20 acres of ground enclosed ... the large cypress shades and pleasant wilderness with fountains, statues etc. have been very entertaining ... the contrivance of the grounds is fine, though their beauty is in the great measure decayed.'[110] However a mere six years later Jonathan Swift wrote: 'It is the finest garden I have seen about this town'[111]. Swift was among the literati of his day who the Earl entertained. He enjoyed cooking for his guests and recounting tales of his many adventures.

When he was 64 in 1722, Charles fell in love with the 26-year-old opera singer, Anastasia Robinson, and secretly married her. She retired from the stage, but to keep the marriage secret she refused to live under the same roof. Charles helped her set up with her mother in a house near Parson's Green – tradition related that it was Vine Cottage in Fulham Road – where she ran a miniature musical academy in which other musicians of the day frequently performed. Society thought she was his mistress until he told his family that she was his wife when he was terminally ill. She nursed him to the end.

After the Mordaunts, the estate was bought first in 1782 by Richard Heaviside, a seemingly unsavoury character who allowed the house and grounds to fall into disrepair. There is a press cutting in the archives from 1789: 'At Parson's Green, five and twenty houses are building each to be finished at a certain day under the penalty of £1,000 – To have these houses finished in proper time, to give the inhabitants a right to vote at the next General Election for the County of Middlesex[112], is the great object of the proprietor'. They are not there now, so where were they? Did Mr Heaviside

109 Denny, *op. cit.*

110 *Op. cit.*

111 *Journal to Stella*, quoted in *DNB*.

112 The General Election in 1790 took place between 16 June and 28 July as voting was not at the same time in every constituency. The law was changed in 1785 to limit the number of polling days.

perhaps sell off the north-west corner of the Peterborough House grounds for these houses, where the 3-storey 19th century houses, 219-233 New King's Road, and the even more imposing 4-storey Nos. 209-217, now stand?[113]

The Peterborough House estate was bought by John Meyrick in 1797. The old house was falling down, so he rebuilt it further east opposite the western strip of Eelbrook Common. It was box-like and rather dull. The inside was designed in the French style, with the rooms having rounded corners. The next owner, Major Scott-Waring, put the house up for sale in 1812, with the sale notice writing it up as 'a distinguished and beautiful modern villa ... within half an hour's drive of Hyde Park Corner. Most desirable for a family of fashion, with a moderate establishment'. The house was bought by William Terry and inherited by his son. In its last days it became an asylum for insane ladies. In 1899 the grounds hosted a Grand Fête and Sale of Work for St Dionis' tower fund.[114]

This was its swansong, as it was demolished in 1901, preserving only its name in the Peterborough Estate developed by Jimmy Nichols for which it made way. Originally from Devon, Nichols built houses at a hectic rate, starting in the west in Peterborough Road opposite Parson's Green. The stone lions on the later houses were his trademark.

Duke on the Green

The pub on the corner of Peterborough Road and New King's Road was originally 'The Pond Head Ale House' (facing the pond on the Green) in 1714. Fèret comments that by the early 19th century 'it was a riotous house,

113 The houses immediately behind them now, at the north-east end of Peterborough Road, were built by Jimmy Nichols in 1888 as the first instalment of the Peterborough Estate, although they lack the later trade-mark lions, as do 219-233 New King's Road, built in 1887. Alternatively, the press cutting could be using 'Parson's Green' in its wider reference to the surrounding area – see the Epilogue from page 59.
114 See further details of the sale on page 21.

frequented chiefly by gardeners from Rench's and Fitch's nursery'[115], on the site of what is now South Park. An extreme example of the riotousness was a fight in which four men were killed.

In 1851 the proprietor was William Carus(?)[116], aged 30, with his wife Martha and two servants. It was rebuilt in 1892-3 as 'The Duke's Head' and is Grade II listed; the front of the building is inscribed 'Re-built 1893' and has a sculpture of the head at top-floor level. In the 1901 census the pub was run by Elizabeth James, a 52-year-old widow; she lived in the house with her four children, three barmaids and a female domestic servant. In 1971 the pub's name became 'The Duke of Cumberland', and today is 'Duke on the Green'. The Duke in question was Prince William (1721-65), the third and youngest son of King George II. He received popular acclaim in England for his role in quelling the Jacobite rising of 1746 at the Battle of Culloden. He became known as 'Butcher' Cumberland, and is commemorated in several pubs round England[117], though this seems to be the only one in London.

Pitt Place

Also Grade II listed is the terrace of houses built in 1795, facing Parson's Green across New King's Road between the 'Duke' and Aragon House. In the archives a press cutting describes some land for sale in 1788: 'To be let, on a building lease of 99 years the whole of the south side of Parson's Green ... sufficient room for several houses' with '4 acres of rich and well-culti-

---

115 The area abounded in nurseries growing fruit and vegetables to feed London, as well as flowers. This one was variously known as Broom or Southfield Farm. Thomas Rench, a one-time resident of Parson's Green, bought the farm in 1711, and it remained in his family till the Sulivans of Broom House bought it in 1823. Fèret calls the family 'prolific': Thomas himself had 33 children, and his son Nathaniel another 32 (though Fèret reckons it was 35), each by two wives! Nathaniel's daughter Elizabeth married Daniel Fitch whose family took over running the farm till late in the 19th century.

116 1851 Census. It is hard to read the writing on the return.

117 'The Old Duke' pub in Bristol was originally named after the Duke of Cumberland, but since at least 1967 has majored on jazz performances and transferred the name to Duke Ellington.

vated land divided by gardens, with high brick walls, orchard, fishpond. House already there to be included if wanted. Three and a quarter miles from Hyde Park Corner. Coach house, stable etc. ' The house described has gone, but the land may well be where the terrace was built.

It was originally called Pitt (or Pitt's) Place, but no-one seems to know the origin of the name. Could it have been in honour of William Pitt the Younger, who was Prime Minister at the time[118], and whose home was on nearby Putney Heath? The 3-bay houses have an unusual design for a Georgian terrace: their front doors are in the central bay, rather than the usual position in one of the side bays, allowing larger rooms to occupy the other two. They retain their original names: Rosslyn, Albyn, Cradley, Sefton and Belgrave. Originally the front part of what is now 'Duke on the Green' was the eastern-most house in the terrace[119], occupied from 1819-61 by Dr James Keats, an eccentric who visited his patients wearing a long, shabby, dark green coat with brass buttons; Fèret comments that if you were in threadbare clothes, you were said to be 'dressed in Dr Keats's Livery'. Alongside his doctor's duties and despite his shabby appearance, he could afford to keep a pack of harriers (dogs for hunting hares), which he ran on Wimbledon Common, as well as Eelbrook Common and Parson's Green itself.

In the 1901 census, each of the houses was occupied by a family with children. The householders were: Rosslyn House - Joseph Beauchamp, living on his own means; Albyn - Thomas Holmes, a 'writer' (which was then a term for a lawyer); Cradley - Charles Parslow, a builder; Sefton - Edward Hutchins, a widowed teacher; and Belgrave - a widowed laundress, Elizabeth Haydon.

---

118 1783-1801, and again 1804-06.

119 To this day the extensions and curtilage of the pub visibly occupy an area twice that of the 4-storey Victorian house.

Aragon House

In the 1901 census the occupant of Aragon House, next door to Pitt Place, was James Wray, a tea merchant. It was sometimes regarded, but incorrectly, as part of Pitt Place. In 1683 the site was occupied by Sir Edmund Saunders, Lord Chief Justice of the King's Bench[120], in what was described by Thorne[121] as a 'cheerful-looking old fashioned house', where he 'took pleasure in his garden at Parson's Green'[122].

Richardson's Villa, from an old drawing

Samuel Richardson (1689-1761), the early novelist and printer, moved to it in 1754, his new country house at Parson's Green, where he entertained his friends, until he died there in 1761. He had composed his three novels

120 At that time there were three Common Law Courts of which the King's Bench was one. In 1875 they were amalgamated, and the title became simply 'Lord Chief Justice', who is the head of the judiciary in England and Wales. Saunders was an honest, clever barrister who held the Chief Justice position for only five months before dying prematurely in his 50s.

121 *Op. cit.*

122 *Wikipedia.*

Samuel Richardson. Portrait by Mason Chamberlin.

(*Pamela*, *Clarissa* and *The History of Sir Charles Grandison*) while living at The Grange in North End Road. Also in 1754 he moved his shop and printing press to Salisbury Court, Fleet Street, where he is buried in St Bride's Church, although he had rented a pew at All Saints', Fulham.

Even after his death, the house was known in its later years as 'Richardson's Villa'. It was demolished in 1805-6 to make way for the two properties, Aragon House and Gosford Lodge, now Grade II listed. Fèret noted, as have we, that the basement of Aragon House appears even older than the rest of it; he suggested that it may remain from Richardson's Villa. It was a boys' school in the early 19th century, and then later a girls'. The other house was named by an early tenant who was a distant relation of the Gosford family. The name Gosford was dropped and the house reduced when the Royal British Legion bought both houses in 1914 for the Fulham branch of its ex-servicemen's club - but the house has now been rebuilt, and since 2019 the name has reappeared for a flat on its first and second floors, with an entrance round the corner in Broomhouse Road.[123]

Diane Patrick lived in a 3-bedroom flat on the second floor when her mother and stepfather ran the Club in the mid-1970s. 'The building was supposed to be haunted by a servant girl who threw herself out of a top window; but she was only ever seen by customers a bit worse for drink.' Diane remembers a regular crowd of taxi drivers. For a joke 'one of them brought in an empty gin bottle filled with water and pushed it to the back of the bar. My Mum put it up on the optic and had sold half of it before someone complained that the gin tasted a bit watery.' In 1928 the British Legion built its Haig Hall[124] behind Aragon House in Broomhouse Road, with space for bands and dancing (including dancing lessons for children). Diane remembers Chelsea Football Club hiring it for a Christmas party. Its walls had murals by the distinguished painter, Glyn Jones, including one of Richardson's Villa.[125]

Numbers declined and the RBL moved out around 2000. There is a visible memorial of their time in the stone plaque on the front of Aragon House: 'Presented by RBL Fulham - "Lest we forget"'. They sold the building to an existing member of the club, who kept the activities going for another 15 years or so till the Branch was around its centenary. The annual Remembrance celebration drew good numbers, but the membership was below 100 and only three attended regularly. The owner hired the bar out to local people or private parties, but the club was no longer viable.

It is now a pub and hotel, under the new management of the City Pub Co. since 2017, and opened to the public in 2019. They have highlighted its historical and traditional associations by calling the upstairs function

---

123 The rest of the former Gosford Lodge (249 New King's Road) has been named Jimmy West House, after a prominent member of the British Legion club.

124 Named to commemorate Field Marshal Douglas, 1st Earl Haig, commander of the British Expeditionary Force on the Western Front in World War 1, and then President of the British Legion.

125 Photographs in Hammersmith and Fulham Archives. Glyn Jones (1906-84) also did murals for, among others, St Augustine's church, Fulham; St Bride's, Fleet Street; and Trinity House.

room 'The Richardson Room', and the basement bar 'Arthur's' after Katherine of Aragon's first husband.

The name Aragon has prompted a long tradition that Katherine of Aragon[126] lived in a dower house on this site in 1506 when she was the 17-year-old widow of Prince Arthur, and before she married his brother who became Henry VIII. Meanwhile there is a rival claimant for her patronage in Fulham Palace, the historic country dwelling of the Bishops of London. It will be helpful to review the two claims.

In fact there is no evidence that she came to Fulham at all. The only basis for the idea is in a letter dated 28 October 1506 from Henry VII to his widowed daughter-in-law. [127] Her health was poor and he suggests that the country air of Fulham would do her good. She could stay in the house reserved for the Spanish ambassadors and they would be housed elsewhere if they came. But there is no record of her taking up his offer. She had been allocated Durham House on the Strand for her retinue, but Henry VII, who was notoriously mean, decided it was too expensive to run. In the event Katherine was moved from one minor palace to another, for the seven years of her widowhood.

She probably never came to this area at all. And note that, even if she did, Henry talked merely of Fulham, not Parson's Green; as Fèret points out, 'it is impossible to assert that this old house [where Aragon House is today] was really the place which she frequented'. There is certainly no support for the definite assertion on the green plaque beside Aragon House's front door now, put up by a previous landlord: 'Catherine of Aragon lived in a manor house on this site in 1506'. But at least the idea is not unreasonable: if Parson's Green had always been frequented by 'Persons of Quality' and 'continued to be the favourite part of Fulham for richer people'[128], it would

---

126 There is some dispute over how to spell her name. She was baptized 'Catalina' and Antonia Frazer in *The Six Wives of Henry VIII* argues that the initial C is more correct in Spain. But once in England, the princess spelt her name with a capital K; so did both her husbands and her daughter; her tomb in Peterborough Cathedral is inscribed 'Katherine'. We are following this usual English practice.

127 Fèret, quoting from State papers.

128 See Bowack's description of the area on page 8; and Hasker, *Fulanham*.

seem a natural place for a Spanish embassy where Katherine could have stayed. On the other hand, it seems highly unlikely that 'the house at Fulham' could have meant Fulham Palace, which had been the residence of the Bishop of London for at least 400 years already, and where the King held no sway. Fèret, who did extensive research into the history of the Palace and its Bishops, never suggests that Katherine stayed there.

In 2002 a set of companion houses was built round the corner in Broomhouse Road on the site of the old Haig Hall. To indicate their link with Aragon House, they are named after Henry VIII's subsequent wives: Boleyn, Seymour, Cleves, Howard, Parr.[129] In common with Nos. 1 and 3 Broomhouse Road, which seem to have been rebuilt at the same time, they have gargoyles of mythical beasts on their pilasters, in evident imitation of the lions in the nearby Peterborough Estate.[130]

129 There is also now a maisonette, The Coach House, in what looks like a garage between Gosford Lodge and Boleyn House.

130 See the last sentences of the section on Peterborough House on page 51.

Epilogue:
The Wider Area

Although we have focused on just the houses round the Green in this book, there were some other notable houses and residents worth comment in the immediate vicinity. Some we cannot locate with certainty, but others are still traceable.

Other schools

In the days when anyone could set up a school with any number of pupils, there were many round Parson's Green. Lady Margaret is the obvious surviving example, but there is also the Zebedee Christian Nursery School, meeting in Sulivan Hall since 1982. And we have already mentioned the 19th century schools at Albion, Elm, Belfield and Aragon Houses.[131] In addition, the Rectory House school opened in 1832, and the 1851 census records 12 boys aged 11-17, under John Roach and his sister Harriet. In 1868 it became a military academy preparing young gentlemen for the army. It gained a high reputation, so that Fèret could comment that after a term or two even the dullest boy would achieve a pass. In 1882, after these 50 years in education, the house was demolished to make way for St Dionis' to be built.

Also on the west side of the Green, Dr George Lambert, John Roach's brother-in-law and a private tutor in mathematics, lived at Nortons House[132], and according to the 1851 census had several private pupils; one was from Aberdeen and three from Calcutta!

At the back of Lysons' *The Environs of London* [133], written in 1795, is an advert for Mr Frampton's Grammatical Academy 'at Parson's Green

131 See pages 30 and 55.

132 This appears to be the name on the census form, but it is difficult to read.

133 Vol 2, part 2.

near Fulham', together with a picture of the building. It was where 'Young gentlemen are boarded and educated on a genteel and liberal plan in the various branches of physical, mathematical and commercial literature for twenty guineas per annum ... and military exercise'. Was this perhaps a precursor of the Rectory House school above?

Other houses near Parson's Green and their occupants

Sir Thomas Bodley (1545-1613)

He had a house somewhere at Parson's Green from 1605-12. He was a diplomat and scholar who gave his collection of books to the University Library in Oxford which had fallen into disrepair, and which became known as the Bodleian after him, as it is to this day. He laid the foundation stone of the new library, but died before it was completed. He presented books worth £10,000.[134] Books were very valuable, so were not lent out; one book could cost as much as a year's wages. He wanted the books to be of a serious nature, so there were no

Sir Thomas Bodley. Portrait by an unknown artist.

134 This and all the other information about Sir Thomas in this paragraph are from Fèret, who does not list his sources. The Bodleian today have no records to confirm the enormous £10,000 figure, which would be worth £2½ million today (Bank of England figures). But in its favour they quote a letter from Bodley to the Librarian in 1604 saying that he possessed 'about 2000' books at a time when it was rare for even wealthier households to own more than a handful; and the inventory of his other possessions (excluding any books) at his death totalled £12,277.10.6¼.

plays among them. He also wanted the religious works to prove that Protestants were right and Roman Catholics wrong. He was very good at getting donations towards the library, by making sure that people knew who the benefactors were. He was concerned that the University should have income, so purchased property for it. He was the 'greatest benefactor of Oxford University of his time'[135]. He used his own money and that of his wealthy wife, whose first husband had made a fortune trading in pilchards. He suffered ill health in his later years, and moved near St Bartholomew's Hospital where his wife was buried. There is a monument to their 24 years of happily married life in St Bartholomew-the-Less, which is in the hospital grounds.

High Elms, later Fulham Park House and Park House

Having bought East End House[136], John Powell built another large house in 1762, designed by Henry Holland[137], which he called High Elms. It was near the junction with Fulham Road at Purser's Cross, about 100 yards down Parson's Green Lane. It was built on the site of the burial of a highwayman in 1738, who threw his ill-gotten gains to the labourers in the fields before shooting himself on capture. A plaque on the wall of High Elms House commemorated this.

After Powell's death in 1784 the house was renamed Fulham Park House, presumably meaning that Fulham Park had become part of the estate; it adjoined the east side of Fulham Park Road, over a quarter of a mile distant to the south-west across the market gardens, and had previously been the grounds of Fulham Lodge. Either at this stage or earlier the High Elms / Fulham Park House estate took over much of what had been the Rosamonds manor[138]. In the early 19th century it was occupied by

135 *DNB*.

136 See page 43. Powell does not seem to have lived at High Elms.

137 The locally born architect went on to design Battersea Bridge, the Brighton Pavilion and Drury Lane Theatre, as well as laying out Sloane Street and Hans Town, Chelsea. He is buried in All Saints' in a tomb designed for his parents.

138 See page 24.

the Rev. Thomas Bowen, who established a boys' school (yet another one!), which Fèret says 'he conducted with much success'; his widow continued it till 1818. In 1850 William Keane described the house as 'a handsome brick structure ... approached by a lodge-entrance and carriage-drive to a flight of steps which conducts to the interior'. And 'from the east front it commands a pleasant view of the park-like pastures and weeping willows hung with tresses to the very ground'.[139] By Fèret's time it was known as Park House, Parson's Green Lane - not to be confused with the Park House on the east side of Parson's Green[140].

Swan House, Parson's Green Lane

This is one house that survived the Metropolitan District Railway development of the late 1870s, and is still standing. It is early 19th century (with an enclosed porch, shuttered windows and cast-iron balconies); clearly older than the Victorian houses alongside, as it sticks out further on to the pavement. According to Fèret, it was originally Park Lodge, adjoining the Park House estate.

Today it is the Ashville NHS surgery, established in 1993. Dr Stephen Aras, the senior doctor in the practice, acquired the house that year, and named it after his home at the time[141] 'for no other reason than I needed a name!' It was part of a larger site (offices and light industry) occupied at that time by Serecol, the paint division of Burma Castrol Oil, but then developed and sold off in 1995-6; the area of garages and back doors behind was named Swan Mews after the oldest house in 1996. Serecol built the modern Lane House in the garden of Swan House, which it now abuts. Swan House was historically 24 Parson's Green Lane (like Park Lodge before it), but the first owner of Lane House had the number printed on her stationery. So, says Dr Aras, 'since I quite liked the idea of a 'Grand house' without a number I let it go!' Today Swan House has no number on its door, but does have a large white swan. Its origin and the change of the

139 Keane, *The Beauties of Middlesex*.

140 See page 34.

141 1 Clancarty Road, also in South Fulham but not adjoining Parson's Green.

house's name from Park Lodge are obscure, but rumour tells of a carpenter called Mr Swan(n) who lived there at some time. If so, he presumably had his workshop in the grounds and ran the business 'at the sign of the Swan'. The swan is similar, but not identical, to the one which adorned, at least until the 1930s, the Swan pub and brewery at nearby Fulham Broadway, itself the successor to the White Swan hostelry[142]; that could be another possible source for this one.

Ivy Cottage

On the north-west corner of Broomhouse Road (formerly Broom Lane) was a curious old cottage in what Fèret calls 'debased Gothic' style. He reproduces an 1818 newspaper cutting found in Faulkner's own copy of his *History*; it is a sale notice that advertises the grounds as 'about 4 acres in the most perfect condition'. The house includes 'a beautiful library ... servants' hall, housekeeper's room, larder and cellaring'; there is also a small detached cottage 'containing a capital laundry'; 'a large double coach-house, 6-stalled stable, excellent poultry yard, pigeon house, garden and tool houses, etc'. It was described by Keane in 1850 as a 'beautiful Swiss Cottage' with 'pleasure grounds to the south with a greenhouse, lawn and flower garden', but he was rather critical of the garden's layout. [143]

In 1858, according to Fèret, it became the residence of Mr E.T. Smith, 'one of the world's born showmen and owner of the Drury Lane Theatre'. He managed (rather than actually owned) the theatre from 1852-62 and enabled its precarious fortunes to flourish by mixing circuses and conjuring alongside the more traditional diet of drama and opera. He re-named the cottage Drury Lodge. Fèret also describes him as 'of "Bloomer" costume fame', but frustratingly does not elaborate. The 'Bloomer costume', becoming familiarly known as 'bloomers', was introduced to New York in 1851 as a 'healthful and comfortable alternative' to the heavy constricting dresses that women usually wore. It consisted of a jacket with close sleeves,

142 Hasker, *Fulanham*.
143 *Op. cit.*

and a skirt falling a little below the knee, with Turkish trousers underneath. It was championed by Mrs Amelia Jenks Bloomer, editor of *The Lily*, 'a Ladies' Journal', and became a symbol of the campaign for women's rights as the 'freedom dress'. It subsequently became the 'bicycle dress' of the 1890s. But what was the connection with Mr Smith near Parson's Green? Amelia Bloomer credited the design of the dress to her co-founder Elizabeth Smith Miller. Elizabeth was the daughter of the American anti-slavery philanthropist, Gerrit Smith. Did Mr E.T. the 'showman' claim some sort of relationship and exploit the publicity?

The last occupant was the Rev. Robert Baker, Vicar of Fulham 1834-1871, who retired there and died in 1878, aged 89. He left a personal estate of £40,000. While Vicar he had the church schools built in Fulham High Street.[144] He was an antiquarian and particularly interested in the history of his parish, writing *Olden Characters of Fulham* in 1857. In 1865, at the age of 77, he had married as his second wife Mary Sulivan, daughter of Laurence Sulivan of Broom House.[145] She was 45 when they married, leaving her sister Charlotte to look after their elderly father. She died in 1871, after only six years of marriage. The Cottage was demolished, and its grounds built over, in 1884.[146]

Broom Villa

On the east side of Broomhouse Road, further south, this house built in the 18th century still stands. In *c.* 1818 it was bought by William Bell the brewer[147]; he died in 1858 and was succeeded by his two sons. The extensive garden has since been built on. 'The Crown' or 'Bell's Brewery' was adjoining, immediately to the north and east, one of the very few industrial

---

144 The building still stands, and is now the pre-prep department of the independent Fulham School. The wrought-iron gateway at the entrance still has the initials ASS for All Saints' Schools.

145 See Pierson, *Charlotte Sulivan.*

146 This is confirmed by the row of houses 40-50 Broomhouse Road bearing the date 1884 on the plaster between their ground and first floor windows.

147 Hence Bell's Alley, which runs between the house and Sulivan School. See page 21.

buildings in Fulham in the first half of the 19th century.[148] Two relatively recent properties, Nos. 1 and 2 Crown Yard, preserve the name and occupy part of its site behind Marlin House, 40 Peterborough Road.

Draycott Lodge (formerly Draycot Villa[149])

On the north side of New King's Road, some way further west than Parson's Green, was the home from 1879-1902 of the Pre-Raphaelite artist William Holman Hunt, a regular member of St Dionis' congregation. Holman Hunt Primary School (yet another one) was built on its site in 1905, and opened with no fewer than 1,148 pupils. The new house-building all around, much of it with multi-occupancy, led to widespread overcrowding. The *Fulham Chronicle* advised the neighbours to suffer 'with all the patience possible' and with fingers in ears! However it also sympathised with the children: 'We fear ... that the position of the children themselves is fraught with no little danger .... Many motorists love to drive along the New King's Road at breakneck pace ... unless some effort is made to restrict the drivers of these machines, trouble in the neighbourhood of the new schools[150] is certain.' In 1991 the school amalgamated with the former Munster School under the new name of New King's School. Our children were keen on the TV comedy programme 'The Munsters' at the time and suggested a better name for the new school would be Holman Munster, echoing the chief character Herman Munster. In 2015 it changed its name again when it converted to academy status, bringing a measure of independence from local authority control. With input from the local Thomas's London Day Schools, it is now Thomas's Academy.

---

148 See Map 2 on page 69. By the time of Map 3 in 1894-96 it had become a Grape Brandy Distillery, and survived till about 1910. From 1905-08 it housed VP (Vine Products Ltd), the largest producer of British wine. The building is not marked on Map 4.

149 See Map 2 on page 69.

150 The boys', girls' and infants' sections were regarded as individual schools. Their separate entrances are still visible in the wall along New King's Road.

Elysium Row

Further west still is a row of 11 houses[151] with a plaque dated 1738 which calls them Elysium Row. Some of the houses have since been altered, and many now house businesses on the ground floor. It is bordered by Elysium Street to the west, and Elysium Place behind it to the north, originally stabling but now mainly back entrances and garages. It was possibly named because of the wonderful view of fields and market gardens down to the river and beyond.[152] In 1866 a severe outbreak of cholera across London caused many children to be orphaned. Mrs Tait, wife of the Bishop of London, rented two of the houses as an orphanage for 30 girls. No. 9 of the Row was the property of Frederick Sullivan, the brother of Sir Arthur, who composed 'The Lost Chord' while staying there during his brother's final illness in 1877[153].

151 But the modern numbering 128-160 New King's Road indicates that some have been made into flats, as there are 14 separate dwellings (we might expect 17, but there are no 132, 148 or 150).

152 The full version of the 1865 Putney Bridge & Fulham Ordnance Survey map (Map 2 on page 69) shows no buildings at all between King's Road and the River. Although Elysium Street is clearly marked on modern street maps, it is not included in *Street Names of Fulham and Hammersmith*.

153 *Wikipedia*.

Parson's Green over the years

Fèret wrote in 1900, 'Down to within living memory Parson's Green was little better than a grassy plot, surrounded by posts and chains. A narrow pathway crossed from Rectory Place to Elm House, while another trended[154] towards the Duke's Head.' Today solid pedestrian paths, shared with cyclists, bisect the Green north to south and east to west.

In 1984 Winnett wrote, 'Around the triangle of the green were a number of large houses, some of which still stand, so that Parson's Green retains traces of its former glory.'[155] Today the 'Hidden London' website describes Parson's Green as 'a highly gentrified locality in central London', and one of the estate agents calls it 'a small patch of triangular turf in the centre of Fulham's desirability'. It is a designated conservation area.[156]

The 1831 census showed Hammersmith to have a population of 10,222 compared with Fulham's 7,317. In the 2011 census the population of the Parson's Green and Walham ward alone recorded 10,813 inhabitants[157]. In this densely populated city of London, our green spaces are very precious. None more so than the Parson's 'village green' in Fulham.

---

154 Apart from its current sense of being discussed widely on social media, the word 'trend' is rarely used as a verb now. It meant here to 'bend or turn away in a specified direction' (*COD*).

155 *Op.cit.*

156 The conservation area also takes in Eelbrook Common. Its boundaries are the District Line to the north, New King's Road to the south, Parson's Green Lane to the west, and Harwood Road to the east.

157 This is a larger area than just the historic villages of Parson's Green and Walham Green. It stretches from Chelsea Football Ground almost to Putney Bridge station, and includes the Peterborough Estate as its southern border. There are proposals under consideration for reallocating the western stretch, and renaming the remainder Parson's Green and Sandford as a smaller ward from the mid-2020s.

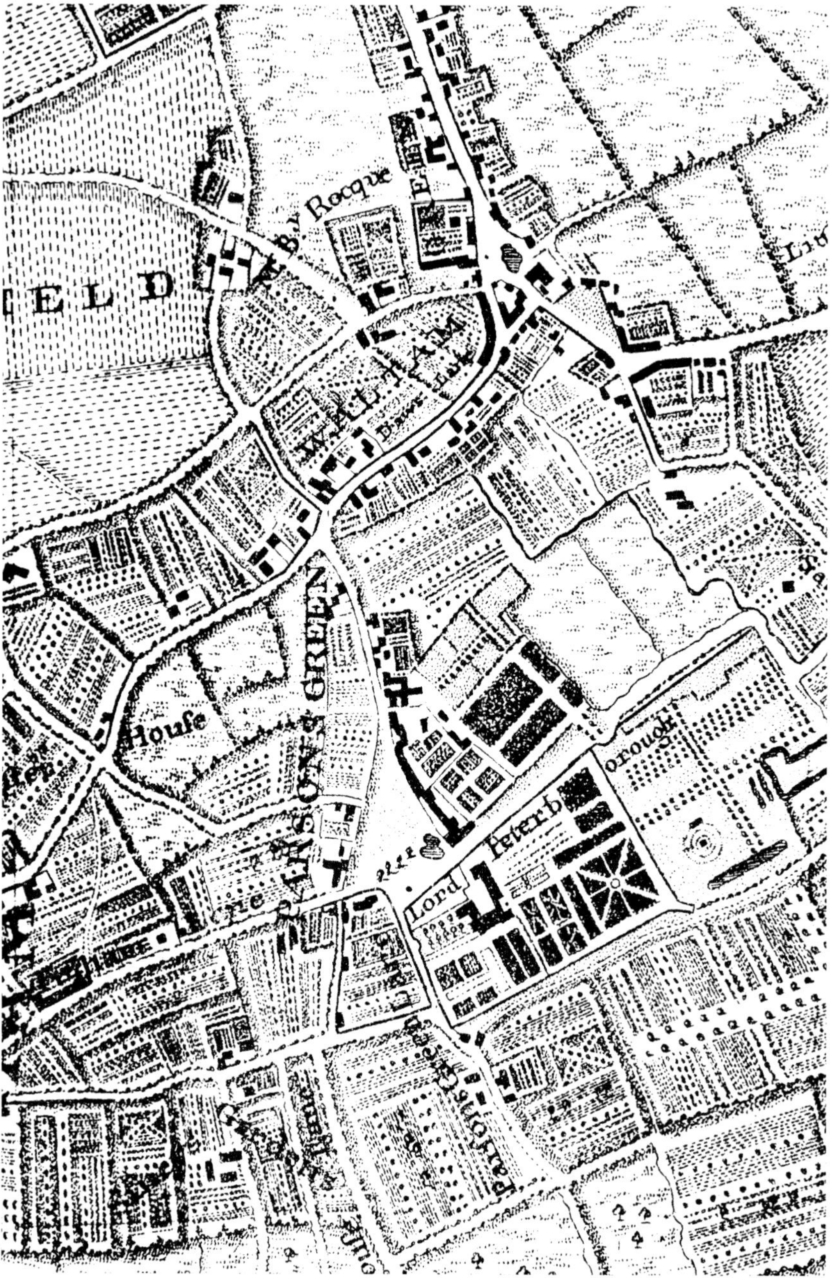

Map 1: John Rocque, 1741-5

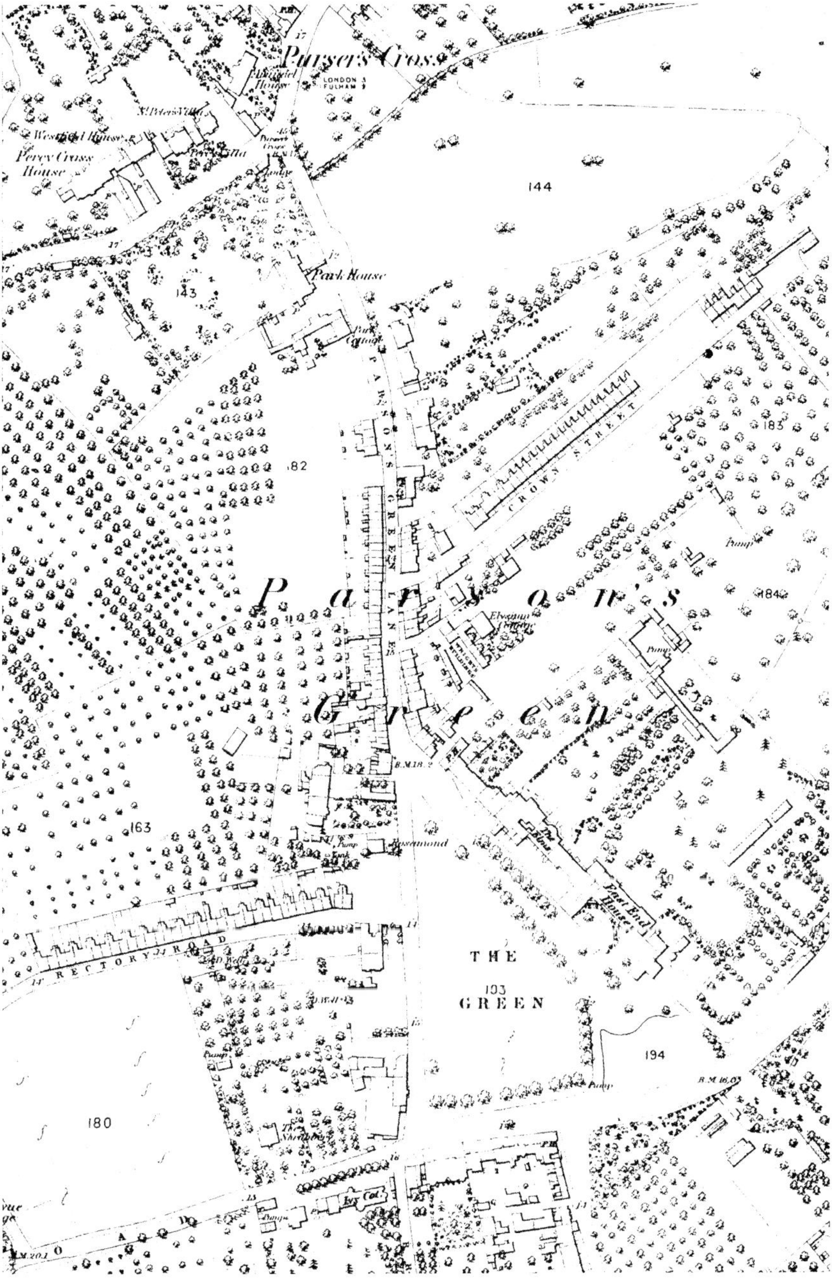

Map 2: Ordnance Survey 1865

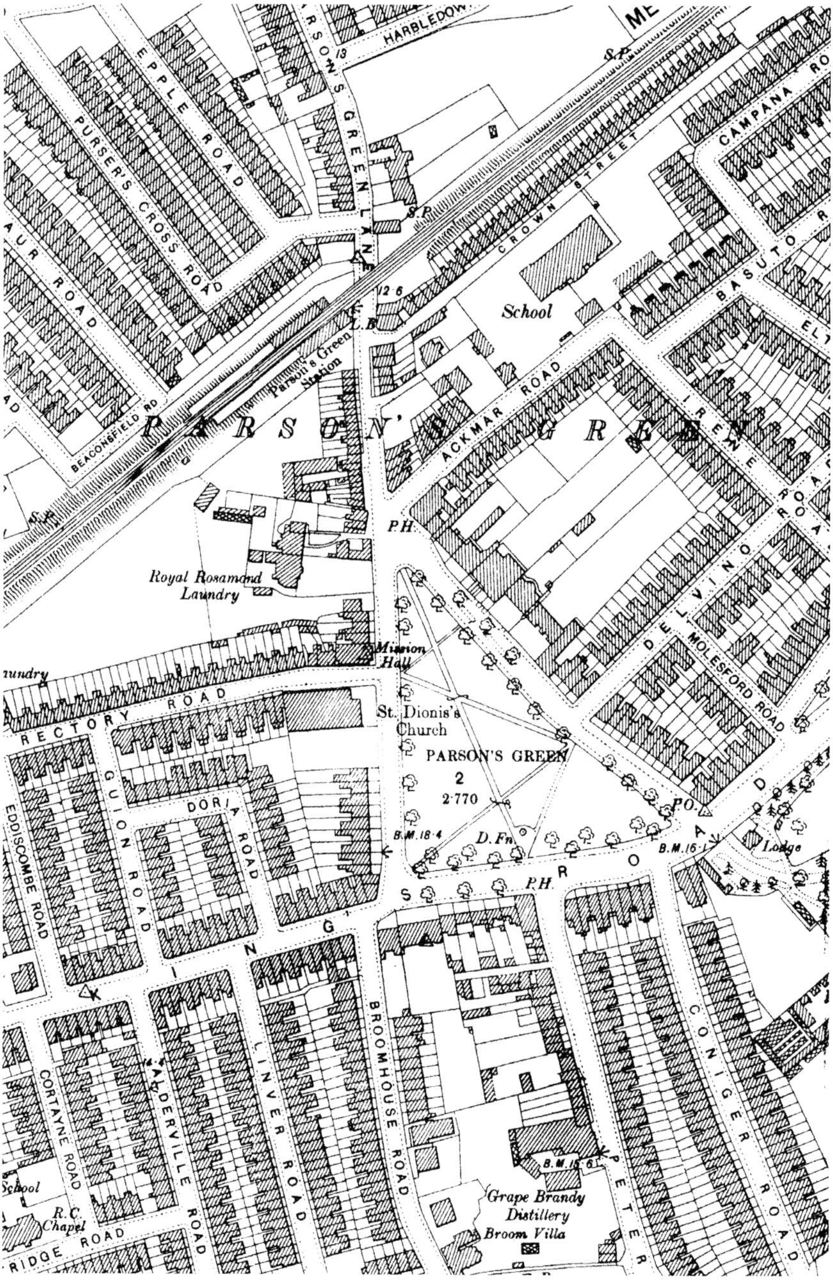

Map 3: Ordnance Survey 1894

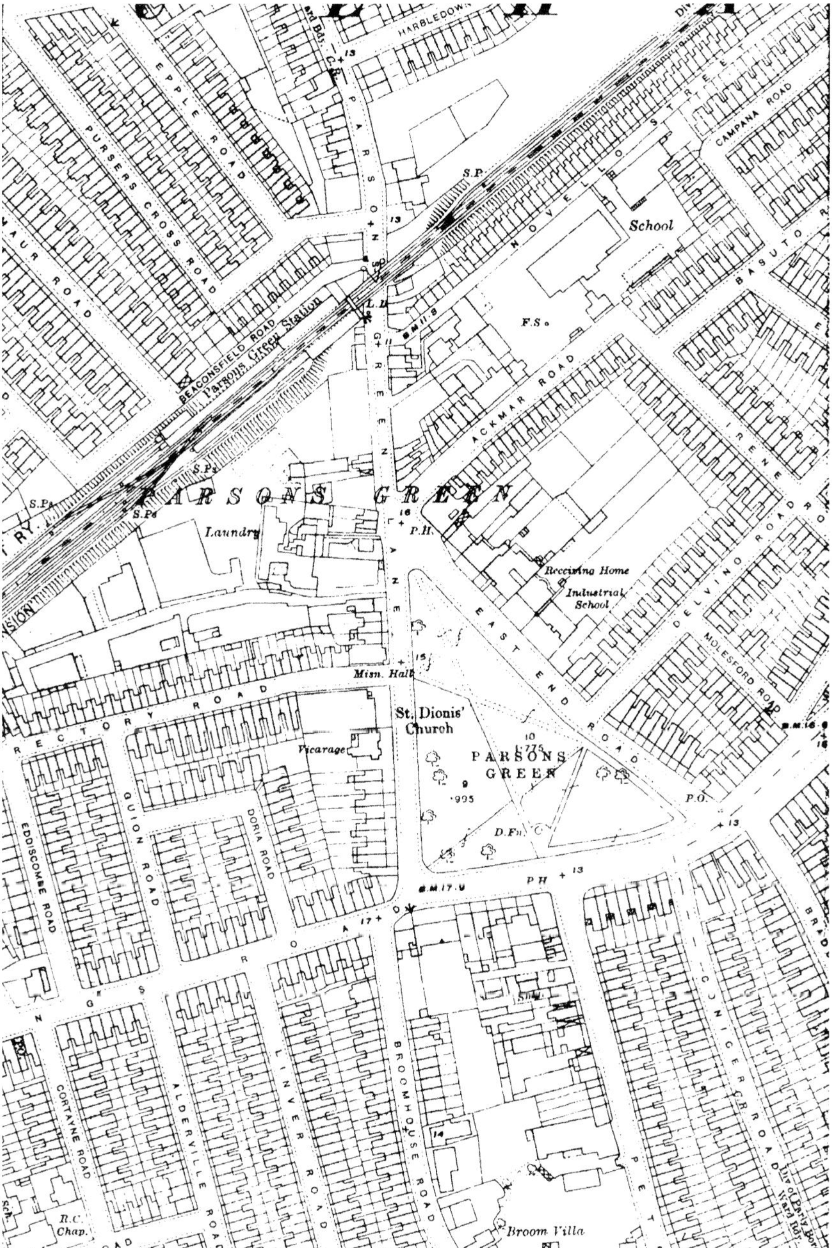

Map 4: Ordnance Survey 1913

Bibliography

Published books (in chronological order of publication)

1705 John Bowack, *The Antiquities of Middlesex*

1795 Daniel Lysons, *The Environs of London* (T. Cadell and W. Davies)

1813 Thomas Faulkner, *An Historical and Topographical Account of Fulham; including the Hamlet of Hammersmith*

1850 William Keane, *The Beauties of Middlesex* (T. Wilsher)

1860 Thomas Crofton Croker, *A Walk from London to Fulham* (William Tegg)

1865 Putney Bridge & Fulham Ordnance Survey Map

1876 James Thorne, *Handbook to the Environs of London* (re-published 1970 by Adams and Dart)

1894 Putney Bridge & Fulham Ordnance Survey Map

1900 C.J. Fèret, *Fulham Old and New* (The Leadenhall Press)

1908 W.H. Wilkins, *Mrs Fitzherbert and George IV* (Longman, Green and Co)

1913 Putney Bridge & Fulham Ordnance Survey Map

1935 A.R. Winnett, *A History of St Dionis' Backchurch and St Dionis', Parson's Green* (Church Army Press)

1939 A.S. Hartrick, *A Painter's Pilgrimage through Fifty Years* (Cambridge University Press; paperback 2005)

1965 ed. P.D. Whitting, *A History of Hammersmith* (Hammersmith Local History Group; reprinted by FHHS [Fulham and Hammersmith Historical Society] 1990)

1970 ed. P.D. Whitting, *A History of Fulham to 1965* (FHHS)

1977 S.L. Velvick nd E.J. Willson, *Street Names of Fulham and Hammersmith* (FHHS)

1981 Leslie Hasker, *'The Place which is called Fulanham'* (FHHS)

1982 E.J. Willson, *West London Nursery Gardens* (FHHS)

1983 *Fulham as it was* [photos] (FHHS)

1984 A.R. Winnett, *St Dionis' Parson's Green: The Second 50 Years* (privately printed for the church)

1985 *Life in Fulham: old Fulham in pictures* (compiled by Hammersmith & Fulham archives)

1989 *Putney Bridge 1894-96* (Old ordnance survey maps – the Godfrey Edition)

1990 Barbara Denny, *A History of Fulham* (Historical Publications Ltd)

1992 Antonia Fraser, *The Six Wives of Henry VIII, Vol 1* (Chivers Press, Bath)

1992 Leslie Hasker, *Hammersmith and Fulham through 1500 Years: A Brief History* (FHHS)

1992 Brian H. Owen, *"... a particularly happy place": A history of Lady Margaret School* (published by the School)

1995 Claire Tomalin, *Mrs Jordan's Profession* (Penguin)

1995 *W.J. Marston and Son 1895-1995* (privately printed for the firm)

1998 Lisa Jardine and Alan Stewart, *Hostage to Fortune: The Troubled Life of Francis Bacon 1561-1626* (Phoenix Giant / Gollancz)

2002 Patrick Loobey, *Hammersmith & Fulham Past & Present* (Sutton Publishing Ltd for WH Smith)

2004 *Dictionary of National Biography* (Oxford University Press)

2004 Chris Amies, *Hammersmith and Fulham Pubs* (Tempus Publishing Ltd)

2005 *LCC Bomb Damage Maps, 1939-45* (London Topographical Society & London Metropolitan Archives)

2008 Sue Pierson, *Charlotte Sulivan (1824-1911): 'The best friend we have'* (FHHS; 2nd edition 2011)

2013 Sue Pierson, *Peterborough House: 'A mansion in every way calculated for a family of distinction'* (FHHS)

2017 *Celebrating our Centenary: Lady Margaret School 1917-2017* (published by the school)

Unpublished sources

Census 1841, 1851, 1901, 2011

Issues of 'Parson's Green, Fulham, Parish Magazine', produced by St Dionis' Church

Press cuttings, photos and electoral registers in Hammersmith & Fulham archives

L.B. Hammersmith & Fulham Character Profiles for the Parson's Green and Studdridge Street Conservation Areas

Peter Kulpa, *Pride of Fulham: The Lion Houses of the Peterborough Estate* (Cambridge University dissertation, 2017)

James Sproule, *History of Pitt Place, Parson's Green*

Internet searches

– Wikipedia, etc.

H.M. Land Registry searches